THE MYSTERY OF

CONTINUITY

TIME AND HISTORY,

MEMORY AND ETERNITY

IN THE THOUGHT OF

SAINT AUGUSTINE

THE MYSTERY OF CONTINUITY ࣿ TIME AND HISTORY, MEMORY AND ETERNITY IN THE THOUGHT OF SAINT AUGUSTINE ࣿ

ࣿ JAROSLAV PELIKAN

UNIVERSITY PRESS OF VIRGINIA

CHARLOTTESVILLE ࣿ ࣿ ࣿ

The Richard Lectures for 1984–85
University of Virginia

THE UNIVERSITY PRESS OF VIRGINIA
Copyright © 1986 by the Rector and Visitors
of the University of Virginia

First paperback printing 1987

Library of Congress Cataloging-in-Publication Data

Pelikan, Jaroslav Jan, 1923–
  The mystery of continuity.

  (Richard lectures, University of Virginia ; 1984)
  Bibliography: p.
  1. Augustine, Saint, Bishop of Hippo. 2. Continuity—
History. 3. Church—History of doctrines—Early church,
ca. 30–600. 4. Continuity of the church—History of
doctrines—Early church, ca. 30–600. I. Title.
II. Series: Richard lectures; 1984.
B655.Z7P45   1986   116   86–7788
ISBN 0–8139–1174–5

Printed in the United States of America

For the centenary of the birth of
Etienne Gilson (1884–1978),
Richard Lecturer for 1937

CONTENTS

PREFACE

THE INVITATION to deliver the Richard Lectures at the University of Virginia in 1984 provided me with a distinguished platform from which to expound the results of research and reflection that had been engaging me for many years, on how the thought of Augustine of Hippo dealt with the relation between classical views of eternity and Christian views of time, as these came together in his philosophical-theological interpretation of continuity. Those lectures—based on the great trilogy of *Confessions, City of God,* and *De Trinitate*—form the first four chapters of this book.

But for Augustine, who was a bishop as well as a thinker (and would not have understood or accepted a disjunction between the two), "continuity" referred no less to the nature of the church. Therefore I was delighted when Seabury-Western Theological Seminary invited me to deliver the Hale Lectures there in 1986, the sixteen-hundredth anniversary of Augustine's conversion. The second half of the book consists of those Hale Lectures.

Like the Hale Lectures, the Richard Lectures at Virginia also made me part of a special "apostolic succession"—not only with my colleagues in the History Department at Yale,

C. Vann Woodward (1955, *The Strange Career of Jim Crow*) and Edmund S. Morgan (1976, *The Meaning of Independence*), and my former colleague at the University of Chicago, Robert M. Grant (1966, *The Early Christian Doctrine of God*), but with Etienne Gilson (1937, *Reason and Revelation in the Middle Ages*). Because my own Richard Lectures coincided with the centenary of Gilson's birth, I was pleased to be able to dedicate the lectures then, and the book now, to his memory.

It remains only to thank my hosts and colleagues for their kindness during my delightful visits in Charlottesville and in Evansville, and my audiences on both campuses for their gracious and provocative reactions.

THE MYSTERY OF

CONTINUITY

TIME AND HISTORY,

MEMORY AND ETERNITY

IN THE THOUGHT OF

SAINT AUGUSTINE

I ୫

INTRODUCTION: CONVERSION AND CONTINUITY ୫

ON 28 OCTOBER in what we now count as A.D. 312—responding, according to his own later deposition in an affidavit,[1] to the heavenly apparition of the sign of the cross bearing the words "In this you will conquer"—the Roman emperor Flavius Valerius Constantinus, known to later generations as Constantine the Great, defeated his rival Maxentius at the Milvian Bridge, and thereby was, in some sense, converted to the Christian religion. About three-fourths of a century later, in the summer of what we now count as A.D. 386 (thus at approximately the same distance from the end of the fourth century after Christ as was the conversion of Constantine from the beginning of the fourth century after Christ) came the conversion to the Christian religion of Aurelius Augustinus, known to later generations as Saint Augustine.

Taken together, as they must be, these two conversions at the two ends of the fourth Christian century changed the world forever and set the course of subsequent history. The political history of Rome took a radically different turn when Caesar confessed that Jesus Christ was King of Kings; and the political history of the West ever since Constantine has been a series of attempts to come to terms with, to carry forward, or to undo the consequences of that turn. What the conversion of Constantine meant for the life of the state and of society, the conversion of Augustine meant for the life of the mind and of the spirit. "With an incredible warmth of heart," he acknowledged later, "I was yearning for an immortality of wisdom," until in Jesus Christ he found the Wisdom of God and the Logos of God.[2] And the intellectual history of the West ever since Augustine has likewise been a series of attempts to come to terms with, to carry forward, or to undo the consequences of that turn as well.

Yet it would be a distortion of both political and intellectual history, and a distortion that still dominates many textbooks and tracts, to stress these conversions of Constantine and of Augustine at the cost of their continuities. For each of them saw his conversion as, in significant ways, a conversion *to* continuity. Therefore the inscription that Constantine ordered to be placed, with a cross, on the statue of him that was erected in Rome commemorating his victory, declared: "By this savior sign, the true test of bravery, I have saved your city and set it free from the yoke of the tyrant, and have restored the senate and the Roman people, freed, to their ancient fame and splendor."[3] The Roman empire had been "restored," its "ancient fame and splendor" had been "set free," its continuity had been "saved"—not in spite of the emperor's conversion to the religion of the cross, but specifically "by this savior sign, the true test of bravery." Conversion had preserved and rescued continuity, and for the next fifteen centuries there would be someone somewhere bearing the title "Roman emperor," on whose head there was a crown with a cross.

Conversion and continuity stand in an analogous relation in the thought of Augustine. A change from metaphysical "discontinuity" to metaphysical "continuity," he insisted against the Manicheans, was not "perversion" but "conversion."[4] In the words of Etienne Gilson's Richard Lectures of 1937, "Augustine was opening a new era in the history of Western thought. . . . Instead of entailing its ultimate rejection the doctrine of Saint Augustine was achieving a transfiguration of the Greek ideal of philosophical wisdom."[5] Thus Augustine of Hippo occupies a place as the great line of demarcation in the intellectual history of the West. More even than the conversion of Constantine, his conversion represents the discontinuity between classical culture and Christian culture. He is best known in the history of Christian doctrine for his analysis of the discontinuities between nature and grace, between man as created and man as fallen; and he is best known in the general history of ideas for his celebration of the discontinuity in the history of the two cities, the City of Earth and the City of God. And yet beneath and behind these discontinuities there lay deeper continuities—or, ultimately perhaps, a single deeper continuity. It is with that continuity that this book deals, setting forth in an entire volume the themes that he managed to bring together into one sentence: "Although we labor, and yet fail, to grasp and know even those things which are within the scope of our corporeal senses, or what we are ourselves in the inner man; yet it is with no shamelessness that faithful piety burns after those divine and ineffable things which are above."[6]

The continuities that Augustine both exhibited and affirmed, not despite his conversion but through it, were of several kinds. Most fundamental of all to him was the continuity he now gained with the orthodox faith of the Catholic Church. "I profess the Catholic faith," he declared in opposition to the Manicheans.[7] And again, *"Haec et mea fides est, quando haec est Catholica fides*: This is also my faith, since it is the Catholic faith" he could now say about the unanimous confession of "all the Catholic expounders of the divine Scriptures, both Old and New [Testaments], whom I have been able to read."[8] For although Augustine, by becoming an orthodox Catholic Christian, was making a break with his past, he was in fact transcending his immediate past in order to establish a continuity with a deeper past.

During his own immediate past Augustine had been an adherent of the quasi-Christian, quasi-Gnostic Manichean sect, which had arisen in Persia in the third century and had spread far and wide by his time.[9] Mani, the founder of the religion, "distinguished," in Conybeare's striking phrase, "between Christianity and Christianity." For, Conybeare continues, "the religion which had proceeded from the historical Jesus he repudiated together with its founder, and Catholicism as well as Judaism he looked upon as a religion of the devil."[10] It was that very affirmation of its discontinuity with Catholic Christianity that appeared to give Manicheism its superiority. "Mani," Augustine was to say after he had turned from Manicheism to Catholic Christianity, "had presumed to be at once the teacher, the author, the guide, and the leader . . . , so that all who followed him believed that they were following not an ordinary man but the Holy Spirit" itself.[11] Augustine was one of these followers, or tried to be, for nine years, from age nineteen to age twenty-eight. His fundamental reason for rejecting its philosophy was his own affirmation of metaphysical continuity and his consequent objection that the philosophical theology of Manicheism "spoke falsely . . . about the basic element of this world, [God's] creation."[12] But that denial of the continuity of being in creation had expressed itself as well in a denial of the continuity of truth.

As one of his principal arguments against his former sect, therefore, Augustine, the ex-Manichean and now Catholic, pointed to the continuity of the church. The fallacy in accepting Mani as "at once the teacher, the author, the guide, and the leader" was that as a consequence "all the testimony you can bring . . . from antiquity or tradition will avail nothing." By contrast, "the testimony of the Catholic Church is conspicuous, as supported by a succession of bishops from the original seats of the apostles up to the present, and by the consent of so many nations."[13] In making his break from the religion of Mani, then, Augustine believed himself to have moved from discontinuity and recent authority to continuity and ancient authority: "I now regard as error what formerly I regarded as truth," he said as he opened his disputation of 392 with Fortunatus the Manichean.[14] He had, he declared to his former fellow believers, found in "the Catholic Church" rather than in the Manichean sect "the most true mother of Christians," and he appealed to them to stop slandering her.[15] If they could only understand the meaning and the source of authentic wisdom, they would, he was sure, "abjure all your silly legends" and "with great alacrity, sincere love, and full assurance of faith, would betake yourselves bodily to the shelter of the most holy bosom of the Catholic Church"[16]— which was, of course, precisely what Augustine had done.

An important component of the Catholic continuity that Augustine had gained in place of Manichean discontinuity was the affirmation of the continuity between "Christ Jesus" and "the Hebrew Scriptures." Acknowledging that this could be taken as "fancy [*vana loqui*]" and as a fallacious argument

5

in a circle, he nevertheless asserted that "the facts of Christian history prove the truth of the prophecy [in the Hebrew Scriptures]," and, conversely, that "the prophecy proves the claims of Christ"; [17] and he seems to have written several other books, now lost, defending the Old Testament against the Manicheans.[18] To his Manichean opponent, "the law [of Moses was] pure paganism,"[19] and therefore not an appropriate foundation for belief. As proof Faustus the Manichean cited the evidence of Christian usage: "Most Christian sects, and, as is well known, the Catholics, pay no regard to what is prescribed in the writings of Moses," specifically to the dietary laws of the Pentateuch.[20] In the face of that inconsistency, how could Augustine claim a continuity between Moses and Christ?

Augustine's reply was a reaffirmation of the universal teaching of orthodox Christians that Jesus Christ had been "the subject of prophetic description, whoever the writers might be, for so many ages before His coming into the world,—sometimes in plain announcements, sometimes in figure by symbolic actions and utterances."[21] Although we cannot concern ourselves here with the profound difficulties raised by such a reading of the Hebrew Bible as Augustine's,[22] it bears pointing out that this view certainly does seem to have salvaged continuity with Israel by jettisoning the particularity of Israel, and to have affirmed the historical character of the Hebrew Scriptures by ultimately taking them out of their history and appropriating them for Christian history alone. For our present purposes, however, this method of reading the Hebrew Scriptures as "Old Testament" must be seen as the effort to affirm that "the God of both Testaments is one,"[23] and therefore to interpret "the New Testament fathers" as standing "in no opposition to the Old Testament,"[24] and therefore as a part of the search for continuity that had brought Augustine from Manicheism to orthodox Catholic Christianity.

Another problem in this Augustinian affirmation of continuity with orthodox Catholic Christianity was the status of the Christian East. Both before and after Augustine, much of the deepest and richest treasures of the orthodox Catholic tradition had been written in Greek. Augustine's great Latin predecessor, Hilary of Poitiers, who had been in Constantinople, was apparently able to cope with the nuances of Greek, despite an occasional lapse in his grasp of grammatical details.[25] Therefore he recognized the poverty of the Latin language as a medium for expressing philosophical and theological subtleties; "for Latin," he explained, "has no articles, which the beautiful and logical usage of Greek employs," and he even anticipated the eventual compensation for this inadequacy within the Romance languages, by suggesting that the Latin demonstrative *ille* could at least partially make up for the lack.[26]

For Augustine, master of Latin that he was, such discrimination was more difficult. As a schoolboy he had, because of what he calls "the tedium of learning a foreign language," developed an intense "dislike [for] Greek learning," finding even Homer "disagreeable."[27] Thus he became, in the ominous pronouncement of Peter Brown, "the only Latin philosopher in antiquity to be virtually ignorant of Greek." As a consequence of that ignorance, "Greek culture did not just drain away of its own accord from Augustine's Africa," Brown warns. "The one man who might have brought it alive there, replaced it by constantly giving and creating," but in Latin and from Latin only.[28] Even before he was converted to Christianity, when he was more interested in the Neoplatonic philosophers than in the Gospels, he had to read them, too, in Latin translation rather than in the original Greek.[29]

Most gravely of all, this situation meant that Augustine as a Christian theologian would not be able, except occasionally,[30] to form an independent judgment about the original meaning of a New Testament passage on the basis of the Greek text, as becomes evident repeatedly in the longest and greatest of his New Testament commentaries, the 124 *Tractates on the Gospel of John*. (With the original meaning of Old Testament passages on the basis of the Hebrew text, to be sure, he was still less able to cope, sharing that incapacity with most Christian exegetes of his time, the major exception being Jerome.) But his having remained little more than an undergraduate in his knowledge of Greek also deprived him of the ability to consult, for his interpretation of the New Testament, what he himself called, in a letter to Jerome, "the books of those who have written in the Greek language most able commentaries on our Scriptures," including above all the eminent Alexandrian exegete and theologian Origen.[31] Such a linguistic isolation deprived him as well of access to not only the biblical commentaries but also the philosophical and theological works of Greek-speaking Christian thinkers. The consequences of that discontinuity made themselves evident above all in two areas of Christian thought: the doctrine of human nature and the doctrine of God as Trinity.

When Augustine formulated, practically for the first time, what was to become the Western Catholic doctrine of original sin, he was accused of having severed continuity with the Christian theologians of the preceding centuries, particularly those who had written in Greek. He was therefore obliged to explain why he was not in a position to "put forth a defense of this opinion from Catholic commentators on the divine oracles who have preceded us." He replied that because they had been writing before the issue of nature and grace, sin and the fall, had been raised explicity by the heretics against whom he was now contending, they "had no necessity to be conversant" with the question and had dealt with it only "briefly in some passages of their writings, and cursorily."[32] Adding to his embarrassment was the action of a synod of "Greek-speaking" bishops, held at the Palestinian city of Lod in 415, which exonerated Augustine's opponent Pelagius of the charges of heresy against him and "pronounced Pelagius a Catholic," declaring that "the words which have been spoken by Pelagius are not different from the church."[33] Augustine sought to vindicate his continuity with the Greek fathers by appealing beyond their explicit philosophical theology to their practice and their worship; for, he contended, "the grace of God, what it could do, shows itself artlessly by its frequent mention in [their] prayers,"[34] in which, whatever they might have said about human goodness and achievement when they were arguing a philosophical point, they had confessed their utter dependence on divine grace. The deeper continuity, then, was liturgical and devotional.

The embarrassment of not being able to deal with the Greek-speaking Christian theologians on their own ground took a different form in the consideration of the doctrine of the Trinity. For although *Trinity* as a Latin term and much of the content of the doctrine had already been confessed by the first significant Latin theologian, Tertullian (who was, like Augustine, a North African), everyone would have had to agree that the speculation leading to the doctrine, the biblical exegesis supporting the doctrine, and the works of controversy

defending the doctrine had originated primarily among the
Greek church fathers of the third and fourth centuries, above
all Athanasius of Alexandria (c. 296–373) and the three
so-called Cappadocians, Basil of Caesarea (c. 330–379), his
brother Gregory of Nyssa (c. 334–394), and Gregory of
Nazianzus, surnamed "the Theologian" (330–390). To this
day, it is to the Greek fathers, and in the first place to those
four, that any serious consideration of that doctrine must still
turn, even if only to refute them. As one of the most important of such modern considerations has put it, "The Greek
Fathers are more philosophical, alike in treatment and in aim,
than their Latin contemporaries. Their doctrine is both more
subtle and more profound. It is also far less thoroughly understood. This fact may perhaps appear surprising, as it is certainly unfortunate, since it is the Greek Fathers who are
mainly responsible for the doctrine of the great decisive credal
definitions, which are all of Oriental provenance."[35]

It is shocking, then, to find Augustine having to admit that
he "does not know" what the Greek theologians meant by
their distinction between *ousia* and *hypostasis*.[36] It is no less
shocking to note that out of Augustine's private speculations
about the church doctrine of the Trinity there came what
would become the principal difference between the Eastern
and the Western churches in the realm of pure dogma, the
so-called *Filioque*, according to which the Holy Spirit in the
Trinity proceeded "from the Father and the Son [*ex Patre
Filioque*]" rather than, as the Greeks maintained and as the
original text of the creed had asserted, "from the Father."[37]
Through that Augustinian construct, the major discontinuity
in Christian history, the separation of East and West, is still
symbolized—ironically so, for it was concerning that very

creed that Augustine had said, "This is also my faith, since it is the Catholic faith."

In addition to these forms of continuity with the Catholic tradition, which Augustine both explicitly affirmed and visibly exhibited by his conversion, however, he also exhibited, even if he did not so explicitly affirm, continuities with the classical tradition; the two most significant forms of this continuity were the rhetorical and the philosophical. Describing the years during which he had been a Manichean, Augustine explained: "During those years I taught the art of rhetoric. Conquered by the desire for gain, I offered for sale speaking skills with which to conquer others. And yet, O Lord, thou knowest that I really preferred to have honest scholars (or what were esteemed as such) and, without tricks of speech, I taught these scholars the tricks of speech—not to be used against the life of the innocent, but sometimes to save the life of a guilty man."[38] He had already realized that simply "because a thing is eloquently expressed it should not be taken as necessarily true,"[39] but he still found himself emphasizing form more than content. That it was that led him, upon being appointed a teacher of rhetoric in Milan, to go to hear the most celebrated public speaker in that city, who happened to be its Catholic bishop, Ambrose. While listening to Ambrose, Augustine "took no trouble to learn what he said, but only to hear how he said it"; nevertheless, in spite of himself, "along with the eloquence I prized, there also came into my mind the ideas which I ignored,"[40] the message of the Christian faith which Ambrose was using his eloquence to proclaim and which brought about Augustine's conversion. And now he turned away from the rhetorical emphasis on form and turned to the content of the message instead.

During the following four decades, as convert and then as priest and then as bishop, Augustine strove to understand that message and to enable others to understand it, too. In the process, to borrow another phrase from Peter Brown, "the huge pressure built up by the need to communicate will do nothing less than sweep away the elaborate scaffolding of ancient rhetoric."[41] Like his Greek-speaking Christian contemporary, John Chrysostom, Augustine marks the beginning of a new epoch in the history of communication and thus in the history of rhetoric, as he moved toward a "wisdom not aiming at eloquence, yet an eloquence not shrinking from wisdom."[42] Yet those words from his *On Christian Teaching* [*De doctrina christiana*] show that much of his denunciation of empty eloquence is itself sheer eloquence. As George Kennedy has summarized the development,

> *Because of the close tie of the homily to the text, exegesis of the Scriptures is an integral aspect of Christian rhetoric. In a sense, exegesis is the discovery of truth, and thus corresponds to dialectic, but it is based on the authority of the message and the desire of the interpretator to make it consistent with the one great message, the kerygma: homiletics corresponds to rhetoric, the expression of the truth to the congregation. This relationship is best seen in Saint Augustine's* De Doctrina Christiana, *which is the authoritative statement of Christian rhetoric, but which was unknown to the Greek Church.*[43]

Scholars who have dealt with Augustine's rhetoric have, for understandable reasons, concentrated on his preaching, but the rhetorical training is no less visible in his controversial writings. Thus in the brief résumé we have of Augustine's early disputation with the Manichean Fortunatus, all the skills of the rhetor come to the service of the Catholic message: Augustine was prepared either to debate "on rational grounds" or to "descend" to the Scriptures, allowing his opponent to choose his weapons;[44] he repeatedly accused his opponent, "Bear in mind that I reply to your interrogations, but that you do not reply to mine";[45] he took a biblical passage introduced by his opponent and turned it against him, because "it makes very strongly for my faith and against yours."[46] And in his attack on the *Fundamental Epistle* of Manicheus, he divided two related propositions, challenging his opponent to prove not both but either one.[47]

But Augustine's continuity with classical rhetoric goes beyond his almost unconscious retention, as a Catholic, of the rhetorical skills that he had learned and taught before his conversion. For in A.D. 426, just four years before his death, he put his hand to the composition of a brief manual on the art of Christian communication—a manual so successful in its own communication that for the next fifteen centuries teachers of Christian preaching went on using it as a textbook. He added it as the fourth book to a treatise he had begun thirty years earlier on the methods of biblical interpretation, set into the context of a general theory of signs and of signification.[48] Punning on the dual meaning of "*doctrina* [teaching]" as both the content and the process, Augustine in the fourth book of *On Christian Teaching* now defended the legitimacy of the use of rhetoric. Rhetoric as such was neutral, "being available for the enforcing either of truth or falsehood," and the communicator of truth should not permit the other side to usurp all the eloquence.[49] He did not go on to rehearse all the principles of rhetoric, as set forth by "the masters of Roman eloquence," Cicero and Quintilian, for his readers could find these out for themselves; [50] but he did apply those principles to the task of Christian communication. Paraphrasing Cicero on the three purposes of eloquence, "to teach, to delight, and to persuade," Augustine assigned the greatest importance to the first. [51] Directly after doing so, however, he warned that it was not enough, in the case of the Christian message, to "teach so as to give instruction, and to delight so as to keep up the attention," but it was imperative also to persuade, to "sway the mind so as to subdue the will." For, concluded Augustine, rhetorician to the end, "if a man be not moved by the force of truth, though it is demonstrated to his own confession, and clothed in beauty of style, nothing remains but to subdue him by the power of eloquence." [52]

Augustine's continuity with classical philosophy manifests a similar combination of explicit and implicit elements, with the implicit ones being once again the more intriguing. The seventh book of Augustine's *Confessions* is an account of his discovery of "certain books of the Platonists, translated from Greek into Latin." [53] He does not specify which books of which Platonists these were, but most scholars would agree that they probably were (or at any rate included) the most enduring masterpiece of Neoplatonic philosophy, the *Enneads* of Plotinus, written a little more than a century earlier and presumably translated into Latin by Augustine's predecessor in conversion, Marius Victorinus. [54] The way Augustine tells the story in the *Confessions*, these Platonic (or, as we would say, Neoplatonic) books carried out a transitional role in his development, and that in two extremely important ways. These books admonished him "to return into myself," and therefore he "entered into my inward soul, guided by thee." But they did not enable him, in his inward soul, to penetrate the mystery of Being itself, until "thou didst cry to me from afar [in the words of Exodus 3:14], 'I am that I am.' "[55] Similarly, the "Platonists" taught him, though not literally in so many words, the truth of the opening verse of the prologue of the Gospel of John: "In the beginning was the Word, and the Word was with God, and the Word was God." But they did not teach him what the prologue goes on to declare: "And the Word was made flesh and dwelt among us."[56] When he did learn not only the preexistence of the Logos but the incarnation of the Logos, not only the mystery of human inwardness but the mystery of divine Being-itself, the Platonists had carried out their mission and (to use a Neoplatonic simile), like the ladder that carries the lover to the window of the beloved, could be pushed aside.

Only they were never quite pushed aside. Students of the early works of Augustine from the period immediately after his conversion have disputed this account in the *Confessions* and have concluded that it was to Neoplatonism that he was converted, rather than to orthodox Christianity. They have pointed, for example, to the treatise *On the Teacher* [*De magistro*], in which the Platonic inner truth of recollection, or *anamnesis*, is identified as Christ the Teacher.[57] Augustine himself sensed—in that remarkable work of 426–27 called *Retractations*, where he reviewed and corrected his vast literary output from its beginnings—that he had gone too far in "the praise with which I so exalted Plato and the Platonists . . . especially since Christian doctrine has to be defended against their great errors."[58] But if the older Augustine thus strove to correct the younger Augustine on the question of continuity with the classical philosophers, it may perhaps be permissible to reverse the process by correcting the older Augustine on the basis of the younger. For in his earliest extant work (or certainly one of the earliest), *Against the Academics*, coming out of A.D. 386, the very year of his conversion, he explicitly affirmed the continuity in a way that he would then manifest implicitly for the rest of his life: "No one doubts but that we are helped in learning by a twofold force, that of authority and that of reason. I, therefore, am resolved in nothing whatever to depart from the authority of Christ—for I do not find a stronger. But as to that which is sought out by subtle reasoning—for I am so disposed as to be impatient in my desire to apprehend truth not only by faith but also by understanding—I feel sure at the moment that I shall find it with the Platonists, nor will it be at variance with our sacred mysteries." [59] That is what he would do for the next forty years. And at the end of those years, as his world was, quite literally, crashing around him in the invasion of the Vandals, with cities sacked, churches burned, liturgy and sacraments suspended—"in the midst of those evils," the official *Life of Augustine* by Possidius tells us, "he was comforted by the saying of a certain wise man: "He is no great man who thinks it a great thing that sticks and stones should fall, and that men, who must die, should die.'" [60] That saying comes from the first book of the *Enneads*, and the name of that "certain wise man" was Plotinus, the Neoplatonic philosopher, with whom, as with the Catholic tradition of the Church, Augustine the convert had over all those years somehow managed to preserve a continuity.

II ⁊

THE CONTINUITY
OF THE SELF ⁊

I DESIRE TO KNOW GOD and the soul, nothing more." [1] This familiar formula from Augustine's *Soliloquies* announces the content of his lifelong quest for meaning and continuity—the self, but never the self by itself or for its own sake.

For the self was a mystery to itself. "I do not myself grasp all that I am," he sighed, which was proof that "the mind is far too narrow to contain itself." [2] To desire to know both God and the soul meant in the first instance to acknowledge that mystery; for since the soul was too narrow to contain itself, and since Augustine found that he was an "enigma to [himself," [3] how could the soul or the mind hope to contain the mystery of God? "The house of my soul is too narrow for thee," he confessed. [4] In the passage from the *Confessions* that would catch Petrarch's eye and "stun" him when he ascended Mount Ventoux in 1336, Augustine expressed his amazement that men would go forth to gaze at the mountains without recognizing the far more mysterious and marvelous scenery that they had within themselves. [5] For if "ignorance is the mother of wonder," this ignorance was "easily pardoned" when it pertained to temporal matters; but it was undoubtedly far more important to come to terms with the mystery of one's

17

own self.[6] In part this mystery was caused by the persistent tendency of the human mind, in its blindness, to "desire to lie hidden," at the same time that it refused to let anything be hidden from it.[7] Yet it was not only from others that the mystery of the self was concealed; "when my mind inquires into itself concerning its own powers," he admitted, "it does not readily venture to believe itself."[8]

It was a common human experience that the self came to a knowledge of itself through the knowledge of others.[9] There were many data in the knowledge of oneself, particularly from infant years, that had come only on the authority of other people.[10] Even other infants could serve as a source for such data, as they manifested, early on, their own capacity for jealousy and rage and thus provided evidence for the universality of that capacity.[11] Conversely, this meant that it was also permissible to extrapolate from the data of the self, as gained through introspection, to a knowledge of others: "All people see in their own hearts that they have a desire for beatitude. And so great is the agreement of human nature on this subject that someone who conjectures this about the mind of another on the basis of his own mind is not deceived. In short, we know [from] ourselves that everyone desires this."[12] Thus there was a continuity of the self with other selves, one that moved in both directions simultaneously. It was the possession of a mind and a body that enabled the self to recognize other minds and bodies; and even though the self was not righteous, "we know *in ourselves* what it is to be righteous," because "I discern something present, and I discern it within myself, even though I myself am not that which I discern."[13]

The self could grasp the mystery of the self because it had the capacity to return to itself. Quoting the words of the

Aeneid, "Nor did the Ithacan forget himself [*nec oblitusve sui*] in so great a peril," Augustine observed that Ulysses was therefore "present to himself" and that his "mind was at hand to itself, so that it could be understood by its own thought."[14] For Augustine himself, this recognition had come in the first instance from his reading of the Neoplatonists. It was their admonition to "Know thyself" that inspired in him what Etienne Gilson once called, in a happy phrase of his Gifford Lectures, "le socratisme chrétien."[15] "Being admonished by these books to return into myself, I entered into my inward soul, guided by thee." With the eye of the soul he came to "see—above the same eye of my soul and above my mind— the Immutable Light"[16] and to recognize its transcendence. The fulfillment of the knowledge of the self, inspired by the Neoplatonists, did not come, however, until he learned to accept the mystery of the Trinity, so that he could, like the prodigal son, "come to himself."[17] He also came to see in himself the continuity of the self, "that most mysterious unity from when I had my being."[18]

The repository of that mysterious unity and continuity in the mind was the mystery of its having been "so constituted that at no time does it not remember, and understand, and love itself."[19] The continuity of memory in the self was the subjective form of the mystery of the self. Yet memory, he soon learned, was of many different kinds: the memory of sense-experience; the memory of what had been learned in the liberal arts; and, in a distinct category because of the inherent structure of the mind, the memory of mathematics.[20] Yet these were not separate parts of memory,[21] but all one memory. From his days as a pupil, Augustine knew about the kind of memory that took the form of learning by rote.[22]

Memory could also be selective, except that in dreams it often brought to surface what one could not control and did not want to recall.[23] From the memory, moreover, it was possible to produce two or more separate entities that had been perceived separately and to combine them, as when we imagine a four-legged bird or (since Augustine and Juvenal, whom he is quoting, did not know about the fauna of Australia) a black swan.[24] Such imaginations were "a phantasm of the memory."[25]

The memory, then, was a "storehouse," whose "manifold chambers" were "marvelously full of unmeasured wealth."[26] Data came into it through the senses and then came tumbling back out of it.[27] Sense-experience collected in the memory the images of what one had perceived, but it was important to note that in the case of words and of literature "it is not the images that are retained but the things themselves . . . , not their signs but the things signified"; for these were, in the phraseology of Augustine's theory of signification, "conventional signs [*signa data*]," signs agreed upon as representations of the things signified, and therefore images in their own right.[28] "To think [*cogitare*]," therefore, meant "to collect [*cogere*]" and "to gather [*colligere*]" from the memory, whose retention of signs and data was "prior in time to the sight of them in recollection."[29] But where there was no obvious temporal sequence, memory had to be predominant.[30]

Memory was, then, central to understanding. There could not be understanding or instruction without the prior presence of memory.[31] "We know many things which in some sense live by memory, and so in some sense die by being forgotten."[32] Therefore Augustine "assigned to memory everything that we know, even if we are not thinking of it." But there was "a still more hidden depth of our memory," where "an inner word is begotten such as belongs to no tongue—as it were, knowledge of knowledge, vision of vision, and understanding which appears in [reflective] thought."[32] For although memory was "a large and boundless inner hall," it was still a power of the human mind and it belonged to human nature.[34] The mind went forth from itself and collected the images of sense data in the memory, which could then be present to the mind as images even when the objects themselves were gone.[35] Some things could never escape the memory, because they belonged to the very nature of the mind itself, for example, knowing that we are alive.[36] The mystery of memory was ultimately inseparable from the mystery of the human will, which could divert the memory from the senses, so that without attention the memory could not collect and retain the sense-experience.[37] The will could also, on the other hand, decide to remember something; for one of the differences between the human memory and the animal memory, despite the obvious similarities between them, was that the human mind could deliberately commit some things to memory by an act of the will.[38] It was likewise the power of the will that "impels [the memory] to take one thing from here, and another from there" to form some third thing not itself in the memory.[39]

A special function of memory was the memory not of outward data from sense-experience, but of the inward data of the self, including the very memory of remembering. For the human eye could not see itself except by looking into a mirror, but it was not so with the human mind, to whose nature it belonged to be able to behold itself without a mirror: the mind "knows itself as though it were to itself a remembrance of itself."[40] Thus while heaven, earth, and sea were all present to the self in the memory, it was also in the memory that "I meet myself and recall myself—what, when, or where I did a thing, and how I felt when I did it."[41] Repeatedly in the *Confessions*, therefore, Augustine remembered, in his forties, having remembered, in his thirties, how he had felt in his teens.[42] "I remember that I remembered," he recounted, "so that if afterward I call to mind that I once was able to remember these things, it will be through the power of memory that I recall it."[43] Memory, consequently, was knowable only through memory. When one used the word *memory*, one knew what the word meant only because the memory of the word *memory* was present in the memory. "Is it also present to itself by its image, and not by itself?"—that was the mystery of the continuity of memory in the self.[44]

As his mind remembered and as his memory recalled its own remembrance of things past, the mystery of the infant mind, and of his continuity with it, became all the more fascinating to Augustine. "Behold," he prayed, "my infancy died long ago, but I am still living."[45] As an adult, he remembered that he had had a "vigorous memory" already as a child.[46] He also pondered the puzzle of whether the infant mind knew itself as a mind in the way that the adult mind could transcend itself in order to know itself, and, if it did not, just when that power began.[47] So it had been that in his infancy he learned words from adults, not by rote, as he was to have to learn his letters in school. Rather, "I myself, when I was unable to communicate all I wished to say to whomever I wished by means of whimperings and grunts and various gestures of my limbs (which I used to reinforce my demands), I myself repeated the sounds already stored in my memory by the mind which thou, O my God, hadst given me."[48] Also from childhood he could summon feelings of the past without necessarily sharing in those feelings now: "Sometimes when I am joyous I remember my past sadness, and when sad remember past joy."[49]

A special part of the memories of childhood were, of course, the memories of his parents, particularly of that strong and quite literally unforgettable woman, his mother Monica.[50] After her death and burial, "little by little, there came back to me my former memories of thy handmaid."[51] She it was who had wanted him to acknowledge, beyond the authority of his father in the family, the authority of the Father in heaven, although Augustine included both his parents when he came to speak about their ambitions for their talented son.[52] He undertook to "review in memory my past wickedness and the carnal corruptions of my soul," as he put it at the opening of the second book of the *Confessions*, because it had been his mother's prayers that wrought his rescue. Since she possessed the ability, not granted to all, to distinguish between the subjective dreams of her own soul and the objective revelations of God, she knew that it was as though a voice from heaven were speaking when she heard the assurance: "It cannot be that the son of these tears should perish!"[53] Thus it was "out of the blood of my mother's heart, through the tears that she poured out by day and by night, that there was a sacrifice offered to thee for me."[54] While he remembered far more than he could write down, he did not want to "omit anything my mind has brought back concerning thy handmaid who brought me forth"; in remembering her, moreover, he intended "not to speak of her gifts, but of thy gifts in her."[55]

Another feature of the remembrance of childhood was not only the remembrance of remembering, but the no less mysterious remembrance of forgetting. "I pass over that period,"

Augustine wrote concerning a large part of infancy, "for what have I to do with a time for which I can recall no memories?"[56] The knowledge of remembrance itself was a part of the memory,[57] but so was the knowledge of forgetfulness. In the remembrance of remembering, "memory is present to itself by itself"; but in the remembrance of forgetting, "both memory and forgetfulness are present together," since otherwise it would be impossible to remember having forgotten what one did not remember. Unlike memory, however, forgetfulness could be present only through its image, since if it were present as such it would lead us to forget rather than to remember. "Now who will someday work this out? Who can understand how it is?" was his reaction to this aspect of the mystery of the continuity of memory in the self.[58] For when something that had been in the memory was lost, it could only be in the memory that one would search for it, which meant that it had not really been lost at all; "for a lost notion, one that we have entirely forgotten, we cannot even search for."[59]

Did Augustine's doctrine of memory and forgetting include the Platonic doctrine of innate ideas? The evidence of his own language in answer to this question must be characterized as highly equivocal. There were things which "we intuit within ourselves," which "memory already contains, but in an indiscriminate and confused manner."[60] Even in perception, moreover, there were "some rules which remain altogether unchangeable above our mind," such things as "the reasons and the unspeakably beautiful skill of certain forms," by which the perception and the memory were in turn formed; they constituted "that eternal truth from which all things temporal are made, the form according to which we are."[61] Like Plato and his disciples, Augustine apparently did regard the ideas of mathematics as somehow having existed already in the mind and memory.[62]

As he contemplated the mind's knowledge of itself, he felt obliged to conclude that the mind did "not gather a generic or specific knowledge of the human mind by means of resemblance by seeing many minds with the eyes of the body." Rather, "we gaze upon indestructible truth, from which to define perfectly, as far as we can, not of what sort is the mind of one particular person, but of what sort it ought to be in the eternal plan."[63] The capacity of that mind to deal with such questions as "Whether a thing is? What it is? Of what kind it is?" could not be explained on the basis of sense-experience, for that was not how such questions had come into it. They were "already in the memory, though far back and hidden, as it were, in the more secret caves," and only the teaching of another person could draw them out.[64] In his early Neoplatonic discourses, especially *On the Teacher* [*De magistro*], Augustine spoke of memory as an "inner word" of recollection—a reminiscence of the Platonic doctrine of the preexistence of the soul, trailing clouds of glory.[65] But his more mature reflection on the nature and functioning of memory, and on the doctrine of creation, led him to attribute this recollection to "the disposition of the Creator" rather than to preexistence,[66] and thus to pay more attention to the empirical basis of memory. And when he spoke of God as self-evident, "not in my memory before I learned of thee,"[67] he was seeking to extricate his doctrine of revelation—and of memory—from the theory of innate ideas.

Above all, of course, the function of memory in the *Confessions* was, in Albert Outler's words, "in the permissive atmosphere of God's felt presence, to recall those crucial episodes and events in which he can now see and celebrate the mysterious actions of God's prevenient and provident grace."[68] Or, as Augustine himself put it, paraphrasing Psalm 116, " 'What shall I render unto the Lord' for the fact that while my memory recalls these [desires], my soul no longer fears them?"[69] It was the mystery of memory within time that "present memory" could hold "past errors."[70] Only in his dreams did the memory of his misspent years assert itself powerfully, "not only so as to give pleasure, but even to obtain consent and what very closely resembles the deed itself."[71] As the subjective form of time, memory could now become for him "the contrition of my memory"; for God was leading his memory to recall his erring ways, in order to bring him to contrition and confession.[72] It is easy for modern readers, after so much familiarity with it, to overlook the uniqueness of the *Confessions* as a personal document. In its literary form, it is one long prayer of confession and praise, yet written, not for God, who already knew all this and did not have to be reminded of it, but for the author and his readers, "to my own kind in thy presence."[73] Nevertheless he was confessing "to thee my shame, to thy glory"; for without the presence of the forgiving God, what would the rehearsal of past sins be but "a guide to my own downfall"?[74] In that presence it could become a way of coming to terms with the continuity of the self by including divine forgiveness within the continuity, and thus of putting the subjectivity of memory into the subjective-objective context of time.

For if the continuity of the memory in the self was the subjective form of time, the continuity of the self in time was its objective correlative. Augustine was gripped by the preciousness of "the drops of time," overwhelmed by "the splendor of time," determined to take "advantage of time,"[75] and intrigued by the complexity of the relation between memory and time. Past things could be said to be objectively "true," even though past time no longer had any existence of its own, because they, or rather "words constructed from the images of the perceptions [of those things] that were formed in the mind" could be drawn out of the memory, which was subjective.[76] The perception of time itself was ineluctably subjective, and yet time itself had an objectivity of some kind, as Augustine put it in perhaps his most famous discussion of time: "What, then, is time? If no one asks me, I know what it is. If I wish to explain it to the person who asks me, I do not know. Yet I say with confidence that I know this: if nothing passed away, there would be no past time; and if nothing were still to come, there would be no future time; and if there were nothing at all, there would be no present time."[77] The perception of time in its passing was similar to the perception of death and of dying. There were three times in relation to death: before death, in death, after death. Therefore it was not, in the strict sense, correct to speak of a time when one was "dying," even though in another sense one was dying all the time. So it was with time itself, where there was no present, but only the transition from the future to the past; and yet the future and the past existed in the present.[78]

For it was not accurate to speak of past, present, and future as "three times" at all. The "three times" were rather: a time present of things past; a time present of things present; and a time present of things future. The first of these was called "memory," the second "direct experience [*contuitus*]," the third "expectation."[79] Augustine found the most appropriate analogy for the passing of time in the mystery of human speech, where, ironically, it was transiency that provided continuity and made communication possible.[80] In the recitation of a poem, all that had reality at any given moment was the one sound being uttered just then, and yet there was a cumulative continuity. The discourse "passes on, until the present intention carries the future over into the past. The past increases by the diminution of the future until, by the consumption of all the future, all is past" and the discourse is complete.[81] And still, he asked himself, how could one speak of the future as being "diminished," since it did not yet have an objective existence, unless it was "that in the mind in which all this happens there are three functions" of expecting, attending, and remembering?[82]

A special problem arose for Augustine in the experience of ecstatic visions, in which time stood still. There are two such visions recorded in the *Confessions*: in the seventh book, a mystical vision described, and apparently experienced, in the categories of Neoplatonism, specifically those of Plotinus; and in the ninth book, an explicitly Christian ecstasy, shared with his mother Monica just before her death.[83] Although it was characteristic of speech that it "had both beginning and end," Augustine and Monica experienced a speech and a wisdom and a reality that transcended time: "And we came at last to our own minds and went beyond them, that we might climb as high as that region of unfailing plenty where thou feedest Israel forever with the food of truth, where life is that Wisdom by whom all things were made, both which have been and which are to be. Wisdom is not made, but is as she has been and forever shall be; for 'to have been' and 'to be hereafter' do not apply to her, but only 'to be,' because she is eternal and 'to have been' and 'to be hereafter' are not eternal."

To such an experience, obviously, the normal categories of time did not apply, and yet it was unavoidable to apply them. Similarly, such a term as *before*, whose meaning seemed so clear, was in fact very complex: God was "before" all things in eternity; the flower was "before" the fruit in the temporal process, but in the act of choice the fruit came before the flower; and sound came before the tune.[84]

The mystery was compounded if one pondered what went on in the measurement of time, by which it was possible "to keep count and reckoning of events."[85] "The periods of time," it was clear, "are measured by the changes of things."[86] These changes made it possible to deal with time as "a certain kind of extension," and thus to measure its so-called length, as "it passes from what is not yet, through what has no length, into what is no longer."[87] Yet one used the phrase "a long time" only about the past or the future, not about the present.[88] Then just what, precisely, was it that was being measured? It could not be a future that did not yet exist, nor a present that had no extension or length, nor a past that no longer was. It could only be "time in its passage, but not time past [*praetereuntia tempora, non praeterita*]."[89] The measurement of time, therefore, took place in the mind by means of memory, in which were stored the impressions made by sense perception as things passed by. Even silence could be measured, but only through the memory of sound.[90]

The reality of time, then, was both subjective and objective. Repeatedly Augustine drew a contrast between the immutable reality of God, whose "days" meant eternity, and the mutable reality of the creation, with its "vicissitudes of time"; between God's "years which fail not" and "our transient years"; between the "incorruptible substance" of God, which was "the source of every other substance," and our own "temporal life, [in which] everything was uncertain."[91] Time was an objective reality in the same sense that the created world was an objective reality, since time was itself a creature: the world was created not *before* time nor precisely *in* time, but *with* time, and therefore there could be no time without the created world.[92] To be made was to be changeable, and so the world really existed but was changeable in time.[93] Like the rest of creation, therefore, time was "neither wholly real nor wholly unreal"—real inasmuch as it came from God, unreal inasmuch as it was not God; "for that is really real which remains immutable," and in this sense only God, not time or any other creature, could be real.[94]

That understanding of the relation of the eternal God as the "really real" to time and creation as not so real because of transiency involved considerable philosophical difficulties. But it was also a source of difficulty for Augustine as a Christian, and that on at least two counts. The first was that the incarnation of the eternal Son of God took place in time and history,[95] whose transiency could lead to the conclusion—which was in the process of being declared heretical during Augustine's very lifetime—that the humanity of Christ had its complete reality only by virtue of his divinity. For the theme of the *Confessions*, there was another and related danger: to interpret the fundamental predicament of fallen man as transiency and temporality rather than as sin; but temporality was the result of the divine creation, while sin was the result of the human fall.

There are passages in Augustine in which he does seem to have been at the point of equating transiency and sin, and therefore time and evil.[96] In comparing wisdom and knowledge, he defined the former as dealing with the eternal and the latter as dealing with the temporal, and explained that "it is in reference to time that we are in evil, from which [evil] we ought to abstain that we may come to those eternal good things." [97] Although he insisted strongly, from the very first of his treatises in opposition to Pelagius, that Adam and Eve had been created immortal, and hence that human mortality was a consequence of sin, he found himself constrained to acknowledge that "changeableness itself is not unfitly called 'mortality,' according to which the soul [whose natural immortality Augustine accepted] is also said to die." [98] The origin of evil, therefore, lay in the mutable nature of man, which brought evil upon itself by sin. Yet as soon as he made that point, Augustine was quick to add that this nature was "mutable, though good, and created by the most high God and the immutable Good, who created all things good." [99]

Augustine was rescued from drawing the potential consequences of his view of time and transiency by his hostility to the Manichean heresy, of which he had been an adherent before becoming a Catholic Christian. [100] In opposition to its assertion of two eternal principles, good and evil, he rejected the eternity of evil. For if evil were eternal, why would God have permitted it "to be nonexistent for unmeasured intervals of time in the past," and why would God then have been "pleased to make something out of it after so long a time?" [101] Since God was one, the Creator of all that existed, evil either was created as evil or was created as good and had existence, if at all, by virtue of that creation. The first alternative was, of course, completely unacceptable; and so Augustine took the position that "evil cannot be in the Highest Good, and yet cannot be but in some good; things solely good, therefore,

31

can in some measure exist, but things solely evil never can."[102] The devil, the world, and the flesh all were evil, yet each, "in its own kind and degree, is good."[103] Evil came through the perverse ordering of our love for things that were intrinsically good.[104] Therefore "he who inordinately loves the good which any nature possesses, even though he obtain it, himself becomes evil in the good, and wretched because he is deprived of a greater good."[105]

There was, then, no continuity of evil; and the source of evil was not finitude, but sin, as was evident from the difference between humanity and the good angels.[106] He concluded, therefore, that "men are separated from God only by sins," not by their being temporal and transient creatures.[107] Time was God's good creature, but it was not self-redemptive. As he reviewed what he had experienced, including what he had remembered and what he had forgotten, Augustine recalled the healing power of time in his own life. He had mourned the death of a friend; "but now, O Lord, these things are past and time has healed my wound," for as Ovid had observed, "It is characteristic of time to be almost a kind of medicine [*Temporis ars medicina fere est*]."[108] As time came and went from day to day, it gradually called back to his mind earlier pleasures and his "sorrow yielded a bit to these."[109] But while time could heal wounds, it did not necessarily cure vanity, which, Augustine was discovering, only became worse with the increase of the years.[110] Salvation, consequently, took place within time, but not by time. For the faith that attached itself to things eternal was itself a temporal phenomenon, "dwelling within time in the hearts of believers,"[111] as the object of the faith was the Eternal who had appeared in time. In the call of God to faith, here within time, the historical time-as-sequence (*chronos*) could become the existential time-as-summons (*kairos*), which declared: "Let it be done now!"[112]

The outcome of that time-as-summons here within time would be the eternal destiny of humanity, as hidden in the mystery of the eternal predestinating will of God. For those who were to be damned, there would be the grim continuity of a state in which they were "never living, never dead, but endlessly dying," the endless prolongation of the moment of death, "when death itself shall be deathless."[113] For those who were to be saved, there was a continuity between this life and the life to come also in this, that even in eternal life "that nature which is created is always less than that which creates."[114] After the resurrection as well, there would be a perfecting, but a continuity, of the same image of God in which man had originally been created.[115] That same continuity through perfecting would also lead the inquiring human mind from reason to contemplation, yet it would still be the mind.[116] In a beatitude of immortality and eternity, it would be able to contemplate both the mystery of the divine being and the mysterious ways of divine providence.[117] Yet some insight into both of these eternal mysteries of continuity—the continuity of history and the continuity of divine being—had been vouchsafed to man as a creature of time.

III ತ

THE CONTINUITY
OF HISTORY ತ

ONE OF THE PERSISTENT THEMES of Augustine's *Confessions*
was his remembrance of the mystery of continuity as this had
worked itself out through the ways of providence in dealing
with him as a person. But he was always conscious of the
broader and more complex context of that providence, of
which his own private experience had been only one minute
part. The challenges addressed to the Christian movement by
the partisans of Roman paganism as a consequence of the
barbarian invasions gave him the opportunity to undertake
the *opus magnum et arduum*, as he called it, of writing his
City of God.[1] Great and arduous though the book was, its
range was "moderate" when put up against the vast number
of "great mysteries" in the historical record with which it
could have dealt.[2] There had been change and restoration in
the history of the Roman empire, but these were covered with
mystery; for "who knows the will of God concerning this
matter?"[3] Even where it was possible to discern what God's
intention for Rome had been, it was necessary to acknowledge
that "there may be, nevertheless, a more hidden cause, known
better to God than to us."[4] God ruled these affairs as he himself pleased; his motives were hidden, but that did not make

them unjust.[5] The mystery had been disclosed from time to time throughout history,[6] but disclosing a mystery was not the same as dispelling it. The God of providence in history was the God of predestination, who had decreed that hidden among the citizens of the City of God were to be some whose destiny lay in perdition, while latent within the City of Earth were some future citizens of the City of God.[7]

Augustine's search for the mystery of continuity led him to the continuity of history, and would no doubt have done so even without the challenges raised by the decline and fall of Rome. For it was inherent both in his contemplation of the continuity of the self and in his reflection upon the mystery of the divine being to ponder the nature of historical knowledge and the meaning and direction of the historical process. He was not himself a historian; except for certain of his polemical writings, such as *On the Proceedings of Pelagius* [*De gestis Pelagii*], written in 417 to set the historical record straight in his controversy over grace and original sin, he did not put his hand to historiography. In the *City of God*, he explicitly disqualified himself from being a "writer of history"; elsewhere he differentiated between philosophical books that proceeded by rational argumentation and historical books that were based on "faith in the narrator," implying that his own books, though theological rather than philosophical and therefore "bound to speak according to the rule [of faith]" rather than as he thought of his own authority, were certainly not works of history.[8] Even in dealing with biblical history, moreover, he could speak somewhat condescendingly of those who "desire nothing else than to adhere to the history of events" and urged that the reader should "raise himself above the history."[9]

At the same time he was highly critical of classical philosophers for having failed to understand history or to take it seriously; their very ability to "understand as much as they could of the eternity of the Creator, in whom 'we live, and move, and have our being,'" had prevented them from making sense of "the succession of the ages" in history.[10] Rather surprisingly, then, it was in some ways easier for natural reason to grasp eternity than time, as philosophers proved when they strayed into matters that were "in the province of historians."[11] Conversely, it was in some ways incumbent upon a mind illumined by divine revelation and by the faith in things eternal to address the continuity of things temporal. Therefore Augustine turned his attention to "this whole time or world age, in which the dying give place and those who are born succeed" only to die in their turn, as the dead were replaced by those who were about to die.[12] Anticipating historical-theological speculation that was to flower in Puritan covenant theology and in modern dispensationalism, he drew analogies between the continuity of history and the continuity of the self, from infancy through puberty to maturity.[13] Such analogies, in turn, compelled a thinker who incessantly probed the ways in which the self knows itself to probe as well the ways in which the human mind could know the past.

It was impossible to know the past "directly" (whatever that commonsense notion about everyday knowledge might have meant in Augustine's complex psychology and epistemology), but only indirectly: "Things that are past do not themselves exist, but only certain signs of them as past, the sight or hearing of which makes it known that they have been and have passed away. And these signs are either situated in the places themselves, as for example monuments of the dead or the like; or exist in written books worthy of credit, as is all history that is of weight and approved authority; or are in the minds of those who already know them."[14] The reference to "written books worthy of credit" raised the question of indirect historical knowledge, whose reliability Augustine defended against the skepticism of the Academic philosophers.[15] But the question was complicated by the prominent place of legends as part of the historical record of classical antiquity. Thus the legend of Minerva's having sprung from the head of Jupiter "belongs to the region of poetry and fable, and not to that of history and real fact." It was necessary to prefer the "historical" to the "fabulous" explanation for the origin of the name of the city of Athens, even though it was undeniable that in some instances "fable accounts for the origin of a name better than history does."[16]

Whatever its source, whether profane or sacred, not all historical information was of equal value. For example, each reader of the epistles of the apostle Paul imagined his face differently; the countenance of the Blessed Virgin Mary was likewise unknown; and even the face of Christ was "variously fancied." But that was not important, for "our faith is not busied with the physical appearance [of Christ and the saints], but only with how, by the grace of God, they lived and acted": not the external aspect of Christ, but his incarnation and humility were "good to remember."[17] Disagreements among secular historians were not to be a source of distress, and disagreements between them and the historians in Scripture only served to corroborate the biblical record as a privileged account and a source of both historical and prophetic instruction.[18] On the other hand, the disagreements and differences of custom among nations, as reported by historians, should not become a source—or an excuse—for moral relativism; for they did not vitiate the unity of law or of justice.[19]

On such a general basis Augustine approached the interpretation of the continuity of history within time. The difference between the continuity of eternity in God and the continuity of time lay in this, that, since it was a creature, "time does not exist without some movement and transition, while in eternity there is no change."[20] It was a series of moments, so that all times were short when compared with eternity, which was "nothing else than endless duration."[21] Biblical language for "time" and for "eternity" was ambiguous and could be confusing; for the Greek word for "eternal," *aiōnion*, was derived from *aiōn*, the equivalent of the Latin *saeculum*, "an age," and yet it did not refer to something that belonged to only one age of history, but to something that "either has no end, or lasts to the very end of this world."[22] The "unbroken continuity" of creatures having their being in time and therefore coming into existence and passing, while not perfect in the way that the continuity of eternity was, did nevertheless have a reality and a goodness of its own.[23] Sometimes, when contrasting the eternal and unchangeable nature of God with the temporal and changeable nature of creatures, Augustine seemed to be assigning to time and history a secondary degree of reality.[24] He had learned from the Neoplatonists, who were "the ablest and most esteemed of philosophers," to transcend everything changeable and to "see that, in every changeable thing, the form which makes it that which it is, whatever be its mode or nature, can only 'be' through him who truly 'is' because he is unchangeable."[25] But he also learned to go beyond Neoplatonism to cherish time and history as the locus of the incarnation of the eternal Son of God within the temporal process.

This enabled him to deal with all the ways in which mythology or philosophy had attributed the continuity of "eternity" to other realities than God. It was inconsistent, Augustine maintained (in anticipation of Thomas Aquinas against various Aristotelians on the eternity of the world), for Neoplatonists to "acknowledge that [the world] was made by God, but then to ascribe to it not a temporal but only a creational beginning"; he was not willing to consider the notion of "infinite spaces of time before the world," for "there is no time before the world."[26] But he was obliged to consider the possibility that there had been time before the heavenly bodies (which, according to the Genesis account, were not created until the fourth day), even though there could have been no way to measure it; but it must have involved "some changing movement, whose parts succeeded one another and could not exist simultaneously." The solution was to make the angels (whose creation is not referred to in the Genesis account) the bearers of that succession: "We say that they have always been, because they have been in all time; and we say that they have been in all time because time itself could in no wise be without them."[27] On the other hand, when Apuleius had said that demons were eternal in time,[28] this meant that they were "eternal so that it may be impossible for them to end their misery"; it did not mean that they could "behold in the wisdom of God the eternal and, as it were, cardinal causes of things temporal."[29] The human soul, whose nonmaterial nature made it similar in nature to the demons, likewise was not eternal in the sense of having no beginning, although it was immortal in that it would have no end.[30]

Perhaps the most ambitious effort before Augustine's to elaborate a full-length interpretation of the meaning of the continuity of history was the *Antiquities* of Marcus Terentius Varro (116–27 B.C.), which, ironically, is now known largely through the excerpts from it in Augustine's *City of God*. Varro had posited a threefold division, and therefore a three-fold continuity, of history: mythology, philosophy, and politics.[31] The first was based in the theater, the second in the cosmos, and the third in the city. Varro's distinction between mythology, philosophy, and politics, or something like it, would also appear to underlie Edward Gibbon's famous dictum that "the various modes of worship which prevailed in the Roman world were all considered by the people as equally true; by the philosopher as equally false; and by the magistrate as equally useful."[32]

The continuity of mythology (and hence of superstition) was, according to Varro, based on "custom," not on "nature" and reality.[33] Varro was willing to acknowledge that if he had been founding a new state, he would have based his theology on the rule of nature and would even have transcended the polytheism of mythology to affirm that "one God ought to be worshiped, who governs the world by reason and design"; but he was obliged "to accept the traditional names and surnames of the gods" because of the tyrannical "prejudices of custom."[34] Augustine observed that in its simpler days, Rome had had fewer gods and had prospered; but as its greatness grew, it felt obliged to add more gods, "as a larger ship needs to be manned by a larger crew."[35] Yet whether they were

more or fewer, the gods of polytheism did represent the continuity of pagan Rome. When someone like Cicero posited a
distinction between the superstition of image-worship and authentic religion, his attempt foundered on that very continuity,
for the image-worship had come from the same ancient figures
whose authority he now sought to invoke against it.[36] Nor was
it possible to demythologize that continuity into an implicit
and universal monotheism, as though Jupiter were being "worshiped, although under another name, even by those who
worship one God alone without any image," or to lay claim
to the Christian veneration of saints and martyrs as a continuation of pagan polytheism.[37]

If there was to be any continuity between Christianity and
one of Varro's three alternative systems, it would have to be
with "natural theology, which is that of the philosophers," a
philosophical theology that had at least recognized the futility
of superstition and image-worship.[38] Augustine joined with
the Christian apologists of the second and third centuries in
finding far more continuity with the pre-Christian criticism
of mythological religion by the philosophers than with pre-
Christian religion itself. In one passage in the *City of God* he
even went so far as to propound the following historical syl-
logism: "The Greeks gave us the major premise: If such gods
are to be worshiped, then certainly such [immoral] men [as
poets and actors, who worship these gods] may be honored.
The Romans add the minor [premise]: But such men must by
no means be honored. The Christians draw the conclusion:
Therefore such gods must by no means be worshiped."[39] Plato
had been bolder than most in excluding the poets and drama-
tists of polytheism from his ideal republic.[40] Yet neither Plato
nor his successors had managed to develop this deeper con-

tinuity with any consistency. One of the greatest of these successors, Porphyry, had vacillated between philosophical theology and the practice of necromancy, which he himself felt to be "presumptuous and sacrilegious."[41]

Of Varro's three levels of continuity, the one most pertinent to the enterprise in which Augustine was engaged as he wrote the *City of God* was, of course, the third: the civil or political. Although theoretically it might appear to be closer to the philosophical, Varro admitted that in practice it turned out to have many affinities with the mythological.[42] For mythological theology and political theology "are both mythological, and both political."[43] Not only the mythological theology, therefore, but also the political must yield to the critiques that Platonism had leveled against them both.[44] Varro had intended to move the "natural theology" of the philosophers to the fore, but in fact he had relapsed into the political.[45] Therefore it was unwarranted "to distinguish the political theology from the mythological, the cities from the theaters, the temples from the stages."[46] For in fact "this entire political theology is engaged in inventing means for attracting wicked and most impure spirits, inviting them to visit senseless images, and through these to take possession of stupid hearts."[47]

Neither the persistence of Augustine's opponents nor his own larger concerns would permit him to leave the question of the continuity of the political order in this polemical impasse. He could not affirm about the continuity of the City of God what he had to affirm without saying something more positive than this about the continuity also of the City of Earth, since both of them were destined to endure until the end of human history.[48] Each city, then, had its own continuity, and yet there was a certain continuity between the two cities as well; despite the profound opposition between them throughout history, they were nevertheless "bound together by a certain fellowship of our common nature."[49] That common nature was the source both of the continuity and of the discontinuity: "There is nothing so social by its nature, so unsocial by its corruption, as this [human] race."[50] Although the history of the City of God was, in Augustine's writing, sharply distinct from the history of the City of Earth, he acknowledged that this was only a literary device, made necessary by the primary purpose of his book; for the City of God "did not run its course alone in this age, because both cities, in their course amid mankind, certainly experienced checkered times together, just as from the beginning."[51]

In Varro's account, human things preceded divine things, because the state had existed first and had instituted religion. "But the true religion was not instituted by any earthly state," Augustine countered.[52] Thus the City of God possessed two kinds of continuity: historical, "as it still lives by faith in this fleeting course of time"; and metaphysical, "the fixed stability of its eternal seat" in God.[53] Between these, the earthly Jerusalem and the heavenly Jerusalem, moreover, there was likewise a profound continuity: the present "state of pilgrimage and mortality" was continued and fulfilled in the "ever immortal" life of the City of God in heaven.[54] Concerning both the historical continuity and the metaphysical continuity it was valid to declare that there had been "no time before it," but that only "the eternity of the Creator himself is before it."[55] The continuity of the City of God, therefore, was not, as Varro had supposed, dependent on political continuity, but served to cut that down to size by contrasting the brevity of human life with the eternity of the City of God.[56] Ultimately, what did it matter to a dying man under what kind of government he was living?

That was true even now in "this Christian era," when the gods of Rome had yielded to the superior authority of Christ, who had expelled them, not from their temples but from the hearts of their worshipers.[57] The authority of the Christian faith had spread over the whole world, presenting itself as "the religion worthy of your desires, O admirable Roman race" and standing in continuity with its deepest aspirations.[58] Even in such an era, the state of the City of God was marked "by goading fears, tormenting sorrows, disquieting labors, and dangerous temptations," as it rejoiced only in hope.[59] The one object for the citizens of the City of God in any age of history, then, was eternal life.[60] Finally, the ground of its continuity was to be sought in the mystery of "what God foresaw and ordained" by his eternal predestinating will.[61] It was the elect city, the predestinated remnant, chosen by God from eternity and for eternity.[62] That had been evident throughout its history, from its very first member, Abel, who was "the stranger in this world, the citizen of the City of God, predestined by grace, elected by grace, by grace a stranger below, and by grace a citizen above."[63]

A special case in the history of the continuity of the City of God was the history of the people of Israel. The reign of King David in the earthly Jerusalem was part of "the progress of the City of God through the ages," for he ruled in the earthly Jerusalem as one who was already a son of the heavenly Jerusalem.[64] Yet just when the rebuilding of the temple after the Babylonian captivity had brought new hope to Israel, the continuity of the prophets in Israel was broken.[65] God had promised to Israel the continuity that "the Hebrew nation should remain in the same land by the succession of posterity in an unshaken state even to the end of this mortal age," but only on the condition that "it obey the laws of the Lord its God."[66] By failing to live up to that condition, Israel had forfeited the promise of continuity and had lost its kingdom.[67] After a "temporary stewardship," therefore, the discontinuity and "division of the people of Israel" had now become permanent and totally irreversible.[68] Not only the promise of the heavenly Jerusalem, but even the inheritance of the promised land itself, now pertained to the church as "the very seed of Abraham,"[69] rather than to the physical and political nation of Israel.

In that sense, then, the history of the Jewish people belonged now to the continuity of the earthly city rather than to that of the City of God. Yet for the story line of Augustine's book, it was not Israel but Rome that most significantly represented this historical continuity-*cum*-discontinuity. Rome itself stood in a continuity, not so much historical as "mystical,"[70] with ancient Babylon. "Babylon, like a first Rome," had existed through its history alongside the City of God, and "the city of Rome was founded, like another Babylon, and as it were the daughter of the former Babylon."[71] The citizens of Rome cherished its "continuity in being" and prized it above all other treasures, including the treasure of morality.[72] As Sallust had said, the Romans were "greedy of praise, prodigal of wealth, desirous of great glory, and content with a moderate fortune," valuing liberty first but then also dominion.[73] In the heyday of the Roman republic, therefore, her foremost citizens had been shaped by "the hereditary usages" of Roman tradition as a kind of "primitive morality."[74] Justice and moderation had characterized that primitive morality, motivated,

to be sure, not by a concern for equity or a love for righteousness but by a love for glory, which did provide a kind of continuity and "succession, in which the dead are succeeded by the
dying."[75] Rome exalted the virtues of "victory" and "glory,"
but these had often served as a disguise for its "lust of sovereignty."[76]

Now even that had declined, and Roman moralists like
Cicero had come to the conclusion that because of its corruption the Roman republic had lost its continuity.[77] There was
a discontinuity of the ancient virtues, and a continuity only of
the ancient "lust for dominion."[78] The republic had been
replaced by the "empire, so extensive and of such a long continuity."[79] Although, in a strict sense, "there never was a
Roman republic," if "republic" meant "the common weal,"
the consensus and continuance of Rome as a *populus* did
come from an agreement on the objects of love and devo-
tion.[80] The heroes of ancient Rome had "found in their descen-
dants the greatest enemies of their glory."[81] For that reason
the change from republic to empire was a deterioration, and
"the very extent of the empire produced . . . social and civil
wars."[82] For, in one of the most trenchant aphorisms of Augustine's *City of God*, "once justice has been abolished, what
is a kingdom but a fancy name for larceny [*grande latrocin-
ium*]?"[83] Indeed, "to make war on your neighbors, and thence
to proceed to others, and through sheer lust for domination to
crush and subdue people who are doing you no harm—what
else than 'larceny' is an appropriate term for such conduct?"[84]
The continuity now was "a chain of civil wars," in which
peace sometimes outstripped war in its cruelty.[85]

Nevertheless, such moralizing about the loss of ancient
Roman virtue, echoing as it did the laments of a *laudator*

temporis acti[86] like Cato, did not represent either the most original or the most profound insight of Augustine into the continuities of Roman history. His pagan opponents gave credit for those continuities to the gods of Rome.[87] To this he responded by suggesting that if the pagan gods had been able to do something like this, "they would have bestowed so grand a gift on the Greeks" rather than on the Romans.[88] Actually, the continuity was the very reverse of what his opponents maintained: it was not the pagan gods who had conferred continuity on Rome, but Rome that had "preserved [the gods] as long as she could."[89] Moral continuity in Rome had not come from its religion and mythology, but, if at all, from its philosophy, which it had derived from the Greeks and not from its own pagan gods.[90]

The ultimate source of Roman continuity, however, was none other than the true God, who alone had the power of granting kingdoms and empires, "giving happiness in the kingdom of heaven to the pious alone, but giving kingly power on earth both to the pious and to the impious, as it may please him, whose good pleasure is always just." In his inscrutable wisdom, he had given such "kingly power" not only to Augustus but also to Nero, "to the Christian Constantine but also to the apostate Julian."[91] He it was who had deigned to favor the enlargement of the Roman empire, when, in his providence, it was time for the kingdoms of the east to decline and to be replaced by a "western empire" even more illustrious than they.[92] This empire had succeeded, as the eastern empires had not, in overcoming the division of the human race brought on by a "diversity of languages," imposing on subject nations not only the Roman yoke but the Latin language.[93] The diversity of languages was not the cause of sin, which came when there was only one language; but it was the result of sin, and the imposition of Latin, though achieved at great cost in human misery and bloodshed, did provide a "bond of peace" of sorts.[94]

The continuity of empires, then, indeed the continuity of the whole world, was to be sought in the knowledge of God (using "of God" as a subjective genitive, meaning knowledge *by* God). In Augustine's formula, "This world could not have been known to us unless it existed, but it could not have existed unless it had been known to God."[95] It had been part of the plan of the Creator to endow the human race, "bound together not only by similarity of nature, but by family affection," with a continuity provided by its "bond of concord" and social unity.[96] If humanity had not fallen into sin, that continuity would have been preserved in all its perfection.[97] The fall had replaced it with a continuity of sin from Adam and Eve to the present, a veritable "concatenation of miseries," which those who knew only the calamities of the present and ignored those of the past overlooked.[98] Yet even after the fall its victims huddled together into a society, a city "earthly both in its beginning and in its end, a city in which nothing more is to be hoped for than can be seen in this world."[99] Within its proper order of existence, however, that continuity of the earthly city was possessed of a good of its own—not, of course, the good of the eternity that attended the history and eventual destiny of the City of God, but a "good in this world," an earthly peace which was not to be equated with the peace of God that passes all understanding but which was also not to be contemned, since it, too, was "without doubt the gift of God."[100]

"In a word," Augustine said in summary, "human kingdoms

are established by divine providence." If someone were to use the term *fate* for the will and power of God in history, "let him keep his opinion, but correct his language"; for "fate" smacked too much of astrology.[101] The teachings of astrology were for Augustine "lying divinations and impious absurdities."[102] It was not possible even to know the total number of the stars, much less to read off the future destiny of humanity from their relative positions.[103] The true God was "Lord both of the stars and of men."[104] Augustine did not want to engage in logomachy over the term *fate* itself, so long as it was being used to refer to "the whole connection and train of causes which makes everything become what it does become . . . [through] the will and power of God most high."[105] In any case, he believed that he did not have to choose between an affirmation of human free will that would deny divine foreknowledge, and an affirmation of divine foreknowledge that would entail fatalism; but if such a choice had in fact been thrust upon him, he would have had no hesitation in declaring: "They are far more tolerable who assert the fatal influence of the stars than they who deny [God's] foreknowledge of future events. For, to confess that God exists, and at the same time to deny that he has foreknowledge of future things, is the most manifest folly."[106] But language about the impersonal necessity of fate and the stars was not a worthy way to speak about the God who had appeared in human history through the personal coming of Jesus Christ.

The coming of Christ was also the ultimate refutation of any theory of cycles in human history, which would necessarily imply that Plato would have taught in the Academy over and over and that Christ would have to die over and over.[107] Whatever might be the nature of the continuity expressed in the biblical term "ages of ages [*saecula saeculorum*]," whether it meant the continuity within history itself or the continuity within the mind of God, it did not mean that history moved in circles.[108] The continuity of a "ceaseless alternation of happiness and misery" throughout time and eternity was not the meaning of the promise of eternal life and the hope of salvation, nor of the Christian doctrine of the resurrection of the body.[109] It would be the very antithesis of the hope and the promise if, "after a life spent in so many and severe distresses . . . and when we have thus attained to the vision of God," the saints could look forward only to losing it all and beginning the whole wretched cycle over again. Not only the authority of faith, moreover, but also the testimony of sound reason refuted the theory of cycles, as the rejection of the theory by a Neoplatonist like Porphyry made evident.[110]

Not cycles, but sequence; not fate, but providence; not chaos, but order; not caprice, but pedagogy—this was, for Augustine, the meaning of the mystery of historical continuity, by means of which God was carrying out "the education of the human race . . . through certain epochs."[111] There was "a certain order of things foreknown by God," as even Cicero had intuited, however dimly:[112] first the Old Testament, then the New; first the earthly promises, then the heavenly; first the natural, then the spiritual; first Adam, then Christ as Second Adam.[113] It does seem somewhat anticlimactic when Augustine, after twenty-two books of the *City of God*, complains in the final paragraph of the treatise that "there is not now space to treat of the [seven] ages" of the world and of human history.[114] Because he did not lay claim to being "a writer of history,"[115] he was leaving to later medieval historiography the assignment of working out the concrete historical significance of the seven ages. What he did work out for himself, as well as for medieval historiography and modern thought, was the continuity of history in the actions of men and in the will and action of God: "God, who is the author and giver of felicity, because he alone is the true God, himself gives earthly kingdoms both to good and bad. Neither does he do this rashly, and, as it were, fortuitously—because he is God, not fortune—but according to the order of things and of times, which is hidden from us, but thoroughly known to himself. He does not, however, serve this order of times as if he were subject to it, but rules it as Lord and appoints it as Governor."[116] As the mystery of continuity in the self, therefore, led ineluctably to a consideration of continuity in history, so this in turn led to the mystery of continuity in the divine being itself.

IV ❧

THE CONTINUITY OF
DIVINE BEING ❧

BOTH OF THE TERMS in the title of this book apply uniquely to the theme of this chapter, as documented primarily from the most profound and the most daring of Augustine's works, *On the Trinity* [*De Trinitate*]. For as the *Summa Theologica* of Thomas Aquinas was, despite its title as a summa of theology, also the most important work of Western philosophy for a thousand years, so Augustine's *On the Trinity* was, despite its title, not only an exposition of church dogma but a dazzling virtuoso piece of metaphysical and psychological speculation. And whatever "mystery" there was in the self and in history, in nature and in grace, in the church and in its sacraments, was a reflection of the first and ultimate mystery, in relation to which all of these could claim "continuity" only in a secondary and derivative sense.

Yet the very temporality of the self and of history, which allowed their continuity to become the object of reflection, on the basis of a Scripture that "speaks in terms of time" and by a mind that was in its own structure temporal, made reflection on the mystery of divine being and on its continuity the most formidable of all possible intellectual assignments.[1] "It is," Augustine declared at the very outset of *De Trinitate*, "difficult to contemplate and to know fully the substance of God, who fashions things changeable yet without any change in himself, and creates things temporal yet without any temporal movement within himself."[2] It would, then, be only "through things temporal" that the mind could be made "fit to take hold of things eternal."[3] At the same time, by a paradox mentioned earlier, it had proved impossible for many thinkers to move from eternity to time. Those philosophers who had come "to understand the high and unchangeable substance" of the divine being have not been able to go on to comprehend "the connected order of the ages" in human history, because they had failed to study "the actual history of places and times."[4] And it was, Augustine reminded himself, not about the continuity of divine being in eternity, but about the disclosure of divine being within time and history, "manifest in the flesh," that the New Testament had used the term "the mystery of our religion."[5]

The self, history, and divine being were thus three interrelated themes of Augustine's thought.[6] As it had been within history that the mystery of divine being had become manifest, so it was within the self that the most cogent proofs for the divine being were to be sought. It would probably be possible to find somewhere in Augustine at least an anticipation of each of the "five ways" by which Thomas Aquinas proved the existence of God, in the course of which he quoted from Augustine,[7] and especially anticipations of the proofs in the *Proslogion* of Anselm and the *Meditations* of Descartes. "The whole nature of the universe itself" pointed, by what later scholasticism would call the *via eminentiae*, to the excellence of the Creator, and the creatures testified to their having been made by God,[8] just as an acceptance of the divine "governance of human affairs" received corroboration from the way it was possible to know even "many of the events of secular history."[9]

Nevertheless, it was not "outwardly," through a consideration of "those powers which rule over the world" or of "the heights of the heavens and the lowest parts of the earth," but inwardly, "within us," that God was to be sought.[10] When the mind "seeks to know itself, it knows itself now as seeking."[11] Therefore the universal doubt advocated by the skeptical Academics was not only pernicious, it was impossible.[12] The mind could not doubt its own existence.[13] For "if it doubts, it lives"; hence "it is certain that he who is deceived yet lives," so that "the knowledge by which we know that we live is the most inward of all knowledge," but also the most reliable.[14] When probed to its own depths, the very continuity and structure of the mind, moreover, proved not only its own reality, but the reality of God: "This thing is good and that thing is good, but take away this and that, and regard good itself if you can; so you will see God, not good by a good that is other than himself, but the good of all good. [We could not compare one good with another . . .] unless a conception of the good itself had been impressed upon us, such that according to it we might both approve some things as good, and prefer one good to another. So God is to be loved, not this or that good, but the good itself."[15] From this it followed for Augustine that "there would be no changeable goods [in the mind or in the world], unless there were the unchangeable good," which was God, with whom other goods stood in a continuity of good by "participation."[16]

Despite such anticipations of the Anselmic "ontological argument," the foundation of Augustine's consideration of the mystery of the continuity of divine being in the *De Trinitate*

54

was not reason, but revelation and authority, which reason could not contradict: "No sober person will decide against reason, no Christian against the Scriptures, no peaceable person against the church."[17] The opening paragraph of the treatise made that clear. "The following dissertation concerning the Trinity," the author explained to his readers, "has been written in order to guard against the sophistries of those who disdain to begin with faith, and are deceived by a crude and perverse love of reason."[18] And after a paraphrase of the creed, Augustine explained (as if he had to explain): "This is also my faith, since it is the Catholic faith," or, as he called it elsewhere, "that which the whole church of the true God holds and professes as its creed."[19] And in the final paragraph of the *De Trinitate* he declared that he had throughout been "directing my purpose by this rule of faith."[20] For the determination of the doctrine of the relation between the Father and the Son in the Trinity, "apostolic authority" would decide.[21] Only with "those who acknowledge the authority of the same Sacred Scripture as ourselves," differ though they might in the interpretation of it, was it possible to dispute profitably, that is, "in Catholic peace and with peaceful study."[22] It did not suffice to give a descriptive account of different ideas and philosophical systems, without making normative judgments.[23] For the difference between non-Christian philosophers, even those such as Porphyry and Plotinus who taught a form of the doctrine of the Trinity, and Catholic theologians such as Augustine lay in this, that while "philosophers speak as they have a mind to . . . , we are bound to speak in accordance with the rule [of faith]."[24]

But the difference between philosophers and Catholic theologians did not lie in the use of reason as such. The full text of the words just quoted from the final paragraph of *De Trinitate* reads: "Directing my purpose by this rule of faith, so far as I have been able, so far as thou hast made me to be able, I have sought thee, and have desired to see with my understanding what I believed."[25] To "bend the mind according to the capacity of human weakness to the understanding of the Trinity" was not a *sacrificium intellectus*, but an exercise of the God-given need to think.[26] In a pre-Vulgate Latin translation of the Old Testament from the Septuagint, for which Augustine is one of our principal textual witnesses,[27] Isaiah 7:9 was rendered: "Unless you believe, you will not understand [*Nisi credideritis, non intelligetis*]." This meant that "faith seeks, understanding finds," but also that "we ought to believe before we understand."[28] To believers it was necessary "to demonstrate [the doctrine of the Trinity] by the authority of the divine Scripture," but also "to such as understand, by some kind of reason, if we can."[29] Certainly it was possible to believe in, and therefore also to love, one who was not known, just as it was necessary, after having pressed understanding to its limits, to hold to the truth by faith alone and "to see it through piety."[30] The method, then, was to begin and to end with faith, but in between to seek for understanding: "Let us therefore so seek as if we should find, and so find as if we were about to seek. . . . Let us doubt without unbelief of things to be believed; let us affirm without rashness of things to be understood: authority must be held fast in the former, truth sought out in the latter."[31]

That method was delivered from rationalism not chiefly by its doctrine of authority but by its recognition of the essentially negative character of all affirmations about the Eternal, by which it was also rescued from the fideism that sometimes seemed to threaten it. Even and especially in his exposition of the Catholic faith about the continuity of divine being in the Trinity, Augustine held to his own version of negative theology (or, as it has come to be known from the Greek word for "negation," *apophasis*, "apophatic theology"), the discontinuity between all thought and language about creatures and our thought and language about the Creator. While what was knowable could still be unknown, "it is not possible for that to be known which is not knowable."[32] Categories of being, thought, and language had all been applied to divine being; nevertheless, he insisted, divine being "transcends the power of customary speech. For God is more truly thought than he is uttered, and exists more truly than he is thought"; and in language about God "things are neither said as they are thought, nor thought as they really are."[33] The biblical promise of "likeness to God" as the goal of the vision of God did mean that "insofar as we know God, we are like him," but only with the stipulation that "we do not know him to the extent of his own being."[34]

It was, however, important to recognize that *apophasis* could be a species of *kataphasis*, that there was a form of affirmation that could be made only through negation, and that "things incomprehensible must so be investigated, as that no one may think he has found nothing, when he has been able to find how incomprehensible that is which he was seeking."[35] For "it is a step towards no small knowledge," Augustine said in his *De Trinitate*, "if, before we can know what God is, we can already know what he is not."[36] Or, as he put it in one of the most memorable passages in his *Confessions*, " 'And what is this God?' I asked the earth, and it answered, 'I am not he'; and everything in the earth made the same confession. I asked

57

the sea and the deeps and the creeping things, and they replied, 'We are not your God; seek above us.' I asked the fleeting winds, and the whole air with its inhabitants answered, 'Anaximenes was deceived; I am not God.' I asked the heavens, the sun, moon, and stars; and they answered, 'Neither are we the God whom you seek.' "[37] The transcendence of God over the categories of time, by which "both past and future with things present are all present," implied, for the doctrine of the Trinity, that Father, Son, and Spirit could not be named in words except in intervals, even though they were not separated from one another temporally.[38]

That is what it meant "to purge our minds in order to be able to see ineffably that which is ineffable."[39] The complex structure of technical terms in the dogma of the Trinity, such as "one essence, three persons," whose different versions in Greek and in Latin had been a source of perplexity for Augustine,[40] could give the impression of a continuity between human knowledge and the knowledge of the mystery of divine being that no one was entitled to claim, as the heretic Eunomius in the fourth century[41] was accused of having claimed that he knew the essence of God as well as God did. To Augustine, however, it was obvious that "these terms sprang from the necessity of speaking," "that we might not be altogether silent"; for "when the question is asked, 'What three?' human language labors altogether under great poverty of speech. The answer, however, is given, three 'persons,' not that it might be spoken but that it might not be left unspoken."[42] To this, more even than to other areas of knowledge, the words of the apostle Paul about seeing "through a glass and in an enigma" applied, as human language sought to speak about him "of whom we ought always to think and of whom we are not able to think worthily, in praise of whom blessing is at all times to be rendered and whom no speech is sufficient to declare."[43] The one exception to the universality of apophatic language was the application to divine being of the term *Being itself*, as disclosed in the word to Moses from the burning bush, "I am that I am": "Therefore he who is God is the only unchangeable substance or essence, to whom certainly being [*esse*] itself, whence comes the name 'essence,' most especially and truly belongs."[44]

In the thought of Augustine, therefore, the continuity of divine being was an ontological continuity. As "Being itself," God was the unchangeable one. "Thou, O Lord, art forever the same," Augustine prayed in the *Confessions*, "yet thou art not forever angry with us, for thou hast compassion on our dust and ashes."[45] When the Bible spoke as though God had changed his will or had, for example, "become angry," this was not a change in God, but in those "who find him changed in so far as their experience of suffering at his hand is new."[46] In the vision and knowledge of God there was complete continuity, and there could not be anything new, "either in place or in time or by any appearance or motion."[47] Rather, because there were "no intervals of time" in God and hence no temporal beginning of the Son or of the Holy Spirit, but only eternal being, all that is or was or is to be "neither has been nor will be, but only is" for God and the Son of God, his eternal Word.[48] That included both human prayer and the things for which it petitioned God, as well as God's decision "to whom he would either listen or not listen, and on what subjects."[49] Although a creature emerged "at this time or that," and thus came into being (as we say), in fact "all these things in the way of origin and beginning have already been created in a kind of texture of the elements, but they come forth when they get the opportunity."[50] God could, therefore, be called "the unchangeable form."[51] Yet this did not in any sense imply a doctrine of the eternity of the world.[52] Scripture said that only God had immortality, even though the soul was also said to be immortal, "because true immortality is unchangeableness, which no creature can possess, since it belongs to the Creator alone."[53] Being utterly unchangeable, the divine being was likewise invisible.[54]

The metaphysical continuity of divine being meant a continuity of "essence" and "attributes" in the being of God, whereas in creatures these were distinct from one another.[55] "In God to be is the same as to be strong, or to be just, or to be wise, or whatever is said of that simple multiplicity, or multifold simplicity, whereby to signify his essence"; for God, it was the same to be as to be great.[56] There was, then, no "accident" in God, but there was "substance" and also "relation."[57] Nor was the continuity only between essence and attributes, but also between attributes. The greatness of God was the same as the wisdom of God, so that mentioning any of the attributes implied all of the attributes.[58] Augustine acknowledged the origins of this doctrine of ontological continuity in Platonic thought, which taught that "to [God] it is not one thing to be, and another to live . . . or understand . . . or be blessed; but to him to live, to understand, to be blessed, are to be."[59] But it was in Christian thought, specifically in the Christian doctrine of the Trinity, that he found a way of positing both "substance" and "relation" in God, both "essence" and "subsistence," both an "absolute simplicity in the Godhead" and a distinct and personal Wisdom, begotten by the Father from eternity, not as a quality of the divine being but as the Son and Logos of God.[60]

The metaphysical continuity of divine being must, therefore, be a continuity within the Trinity, where "the working of Father and Son is indivisible."[61] It was the trinitarian doctrine of the eternal preexistence of the Logos and Son of God that enabled Augustine to clarify the relation between time and existence. The saying of the psalm, "Before the dawn I begat thee," meant, "before all times and temporal things."[62] For the Father spoke the Word that was his Logos and Son, not in a sequence "through certain spaces of time," as a sentence was pronounced, but eternally.[63] It was a contradiction in terms to say, as heretics did, that "if he is a Son, then he was born, and if he was born, there was a time when the Son was not."[64] For time had been at all times, since there was no time without time, but time was a creature and was not coeternal with God; conversely, God the Trinity "was before [creatures] though at no time without them, because he preceded them, not by the lapse of time but by his abiding eternity."[65] In an argument set forth also by Athanasius,[66] Augustine insisted that the term *Father* was not a metaphor when applied to God but that it was a metaphor when applied to anyone but God, since all human "fathers" themselves had had fathers in turn, while "every kind of paternity in heaven and on earth takes its name from the Father" of Jesus Christ.[67] Similarly, it was a hermeneutical axiom concerning two different kinds of continuity that the term *one* could refer either to two or more entities that were "one" in person but distinct in nature, as soul and body were, or "one" in nature but distinct in person, as Father, Son, and Holy Spirit were; failure to observe this axiom would lead to grave misunderstandings of the continuity within the Trinity.[68]

A corollary axiom provided a method for dealing with biblical language, which was "apparently contradictory" about the continuity and discontinuity between God the Father and God the Son: "We are to distinguish what relates to the 'form of God,' in which [the Son] is equal to the Father, and what to the 'form of a servant' which he took, in which he is less than the Father."[69] Read backwards from the days of his flesh, this continuity meant that the theophanies of Old Testament history were to be seen as trinitarian manifestations, and some of them "not unfitly" as prefigurations of the incarnation, "either testimonies of the mission [of the Son of God in time] or the mission itself."[70] Read forwards from the days of his flesh, there was a continuity between the earthly, historical appearance of the Son of God and his return to judgment; for he would "judge as Son of man, yet not by human power."[71] There was likewise a continuity of the reign of Christ: the language of the New Testament about his reigning until "he delivers the kingdom to God the Father" must be taken to mean "that he does not take it away from himself."[72]

To this understanding of the metaphysical continuity within the Trinity, much of which he shared with Catholic orthodoxy East and West in the fourth and fifth centuries, Augustine did add a special theme of his own: the ontological place of the Holy Spirit as guarantor of continuity. In the inner life of the Holy Trinity, the Father loved the Son and the Son loved the Father, but the Love wherewith they loved each other was the Holy Spirit; for "if this [Love] is nothing, how is God called 'love,' and if it is not [divine] essence, how is God 'essence'?"[73] God was holy and God was spirit, yet the Holy Spirit was specifically called by those generally divine terms because there was a sense in which the Holy Spirit was the "holiness," perhaps also the "goodness," shared by the Father and the Son. This was an explicitly trinitarian answer to what was implicitly

a trinitarian question: "Who made the world [God the Cre-
ator], by what means [God the Word], and why [because it
was good, in God the Holy Spirit]?"[74] And so when the New
Testament admonished believers "to maintain the unity of the
Spirit in the bond of peace," it was propounding an image and
an imitation of the continuity within the Trinity, where the
Spirit was the unity maintained by the Father and the Son with
each other.[75]

If, then, the Holy Spirit performed this metaphysical function as the "bond of peace" within the Trinity, it seemed to
follow necessarily that "the Holy Spirit proceeds also from
[the Son]," not only from the Father[76]—the notorious doctrine of *ex Patre Filioque*, over which the Eastern and Western
churches have been disputing for a thousand years.[77] Quite
apart from its status as a dogma or as a point of schism, however, this identification of the Holy Spirit as the Love binding
the Father to the Son within the unity of the Trinity was Augustine's way of emphasizing that, as he himself put it, "no
other thing is chiefly to be regarded in this inquiry which we
are making concerning the Trinity and concerning the knowledge of God than what is true, or rather, what is love."[78] The
definition of love as the continuity within the divine being
of the Trinity was inseparable from the identification of love
as the locus of continuity between the divine being and human life; for "we love God and our neighbor from one and
the same love, but we love God for the sake of God, and ourselves and our neighbors for the sake of God."[79] Thus when
it moved from "ontology" to "economy," from the eternal
metaphysical reality of the unchangeable God to the temporal realms of the self and of history, Augustine's trinitarian
doctrine of the continuity of divine being confirmed both the

image of the Trinity as memory within the self and the manifestation of the Trinity within history through the incarnation.

If the doctrine of *Filioque* was the most ecumenically fateful of Augustine's speculations about the Trinity, the most audacious and (to use a word that he would almost certainly have despised) "creative" of these speculations was the proposal that the "image of God," that primary sign of continuity between Creator and creature, was in fact an *imago Trinitatis* built into the human self and the human psyche.[80] The words of the creation story, "Let *us* make man after *our* image," had long been taken by Christian exegetes as proof that the doctrine of God as Trinity was present already in the Old Testament—an exegesis that Augustine shared, of course, together with the identification of the Son of God as "the [metaphysical] image of the Father."[81] But he was impelled to reject the interpretation of "our image" which held that man had been created after the image of any one person of the Trinity;[82] and at the end of the seventh book of *De Trinitate*, after his lengthy rehearsal of the traditional proof texts for the orthodox doctrine of the Trinity, including these words of the creation story, he concluded: "The Father, and Son, and Holy Spirit make [man] after the image of Father, and Son, and Holy Spirit, that man might subsist after the image of God. And God is the Trinity. . . . Man is said to be 'after the image,' on account . . . of the inequality of the likeness; and therefore after *our* image, that man might be the image of the Trinity; not equal to the Trinity as the Son is equal to the Father, but approaching to it . . . by a certain likeness."[83] Most of the balance of the treatise is dedicated to pursuing that likeness and continuity.

There were some suggestions of trinitarian continuity, such as the "trinity" of father, mother, and child, that could be rejected as patently "absurd" and "false."[84] Others—such as the one proposed already in the *Confessions*, "to be, to know, and to will";[85] or one proposed in the *City of God*, consisting of our existence, our knowledge, and our love of both[86]—were much more promising. For it was the testimony both of apostolic authority and of sound reason that "man was made in the image of God not according to the shape of his body, but according to his rational mind."[87] The image of God was "the little spark of reason, which has not quite been quenched" and which gave man dominion over the irrational creation, though not over other rational creatures.[88] Looking for the signs of the divine Trinity in a trinity within the mind necessarily involved the whole mind, "the action of the reason in things temporal" no less than "the contemplation of things eternal," the "outer man" no less than the "inner man."[89] It was, nevertheless, this "inner man" who was in a special sense "conformed to the image of the Son of God," whereas a preoccupation with "the trinity of the outer man" could produce a degenerate rather than a holy life.[90] Therefore Augustine's analysis of the trinitarian structure of love as entailing "one that loves, and one that is loved, and love itself" could become for him "the hinge of some starting point from which to weave the rest of our discourse."[91] And as becomes evident from a consideration of his idea of the Holy Spirit as the personal Love by which the Father and the Son loved each other, this "hinge" could lead to important insights.[92]

Yet the most fruitful line of inquiry in Augustine's search for the continuity of divine being with a human trinity took him back to the central theme of the *Confessions*, the mystery of continuity in memory. "The three terms, memory, intelligence, will," which were distinct from one another and yet were not three lives in man or three minds, but one life and one mind, themselves intimated "a trinity of the mind," in which each corresponded to one of the persons of the divine Trinity.[93] But of the three, it was memory that took Augustine the furthest in his analysis; for memory "is called life, and mind, and substance in relation to itself, but is called memory in relation to something else ..., [because] I remember that I have memory."[94] The effort to probe the inner life by abstracting away the forms of the body and of sense experience demonstrated the continuity of memory.[95] Every act of remembering "proceeds [, first,] from those things which are retained in the memory, with the addition [, second,] also of those which, by the act of discerning, are copied thence through recollection," as these were combined [, third,] by the will; and yet the three were one. There are, Augustine suggested, "as many trinities of this kind as there are remembrances."[96]

Promising and fruitful though it was, the application of the notion of memory to a consideration of the continuity of divine being was fraught with peril. Therefore Augustine opened *De Trinitate*, his exploration of the analogies between the human mind and the divine Trinity, with a specific warning about the anthropopathism of this particular analogy, and he returned to this warning when he showed how the analogy broke down.[97] God did not have to be reminded of anything, and the biblical image of "the book of life" did not refer to a divine mnemomic device, but to "his infallible prescience" of everything that was to happen.[98] The "memory" of God in relation to humanity, then, was a way of speaking

66

about the forgiving compassion of God.[99] Nevertheless, there was a proper way of attributing memory to the mystery of the Trinity, indeed to the persons in the Trinity, so that the Father remembered himself and the Son, and the Son likewise remembered the Father and himself.[100] Conversely, the idea that God could be in the human memory was also mysterious: "Where in my memory dost thou abide, O Lord?" he asked in the *Confessions*.[101] Still it lay within the capacity of the human mind, and was its "special wretchedness," that it could even forget God and thus "not be with him without whom it cannot be," and yet also that it could remember God.[102]

Memory had one additional advantage as a true image in continuity with the Trinity: in one sense it was temporal, but in another sense it was eternal; for it was not simply the memory of itself or of anything human, but "the remembrance, understanding, and love of him by whom it was made."[103] Being temporal and yet eternal, the memory also represented the relation of the eternal God to time and history, established when the one who was eternally "light from light" became incarnate "from a certain time," so that "we may turn ourselves to him in time, that is, from some particular time."[104] "Wisdom" consisted in the knowledge of eternity in the Logos, "knowledge" in the knowledge of time in the Incarnate One; for the opening words of the prologue to the Gospel of John, "In the beginning was the Word," dealt with eternity, but then it went on, "The Word was made flesh," to deal with time.[105] In interpreting the theophanies of the Old Testament it was possible to speak of a use of created mediators such as angels by the unchangeable and eternal Creator, as it was possible to speak of the Holy Spirit's having become manifest through the "temporal motions" of some "subjected and subservient creature" such as the dove at Christ's baptism or the tongues of fire at Pentecost, without the formation of any personal union between Creator and creature.[106] But that was not sufficient to characterize what had happened in the coming of Jesus Christ, which required that both the eternity of the Word and the temporality of the incarnation of the Word, both his continuity with the eternal being of God and his continuity with the temporal being of man, be taken with utmost seriousness:

> *Therefore, since without any commencement of time, the Word was in the beginning . . . it was for the Word itself without any time {to determine} at what time the Word was to be made flesh and dwell among us. And when this fullness of time had come, "God sent forth his Son, made of a woman," that is, made in time, that the Incarnate Word might appear to men; while it was for that Word himself, apart from time, {to determine} at what time this was to be done. For the order of times is in the eternal wisdom of God without time.*[107]

To this historical time-as-sequence of God's action (*chronos*) there must be added the existential time-as-summons (*kairos*);[108] for while time could be predicated of God only metaphorically, it was nevertheless true that "to be the Lord of man happened to God in time," and "certainly to be your Lord, or mine, happened to God in time."[109] The continuity of the self and the continuity of history were ultimately grounded in the continuity of divine being, but this in turn had found its scope and had achieved its goal only through the mystery of continuity that made itself visible in the human self and in human history, both through nature and through grace.

V &

NATURE AND GRACE
IN CONTINUITY AND
DISCONTINUITY &

IN THE CHECKERED HISTORY of the philosophical speculation about the dialectical relation between free will and necessity, and thus of the (related, though not identical) theological speculation about the dialectical relation between nature
and grace, Augustine occupies a fortunate place—or, as he
would certainly have preferred to say, a providential place.[1]
As he was to discover to his chagrin,[2] most Christian thinkers
before him, Western but especially Eastern, had seen the
principal threat to the dialectic as coming from determinism
and fatalism, and had therefore cast themselves in the role of
defenders of nature and of free will against this threat rather
than defenders of grace against the threat of an excessive
reliance on natural human capacity. By contrast, the Protestant Reformers Luther and Calvin, often laying explicit
claim to a continuity with Augustine—as Calvin said,
"Augustine is completely on our side"[3]—perceived the situation in diametrically opposite fashion: for them the threat
came from an emphasis on nature and free will that reduced
the importance of grace, and therefore grace had to be exalted
over nature in the dialectic, even if this entailed surrendering
or sharply curtailing the doctrine of the freedom of the will.

What makes Augustine almost unique is that in the course of his lifetime he had the opportunity and the obligation to face equal threats from both poles of the dialectic—not indeed simultaneously, but successively. For first as an adherent of the deterministic theories of Manicheism and then as an opponent of those theories, he spent more than a decade of his early adult life confronting what he perceived to be an exclusive emphasis on necessity; and he spent more than a decade at the end of his life contending against what he believed to be a grave excess of generosity toward free will in the theories of his Pelagian opponents. And he therefore formulated his own theories about free will and necessity in the setting of detailed attention both to the continuity and to the discontinuity between nature and grace. He did so successively, but that does not automatically guarantee that he did so successfully; indeed, his opponents on all sides were quite sure that he had not been successful. And even a highly sympathetic modern editor of his works has suggested that this war on two fronts, far from having been enabled him to recognize the dialectical relation between freedom and necessity, nature and grace, caused him to fall into exaggerations both times: "The fact is, that in the Anti-Manichaean time he went too far in maintaining the absolute freedom of the will and the impossibility of sin apart from personal will in the sinner; while in the Anti-Pelagian time he ventured too near to the fatalism that he so earnestly combated in the Manichaeans."[4] Many of the same issues—moral and practical, as well as theoretical and metaphysical[5]—arose in both the Manichean and the Pelagian controversies of Augustine, compelling him to look at nature and grace in polarity. Without imposing an arbitrary symmetry on his thought, but rather finding connections that are already there in the material, it seems appropriate to examine the same set of issues twice in looking at this polarity.

At the center of his case against Manichean dualism Augustine put the question of nature, or being, or essence. In a comment that is interesting also for the history of Latin philosophical vocabulary,[6] he explained: " 'Nature [*natura*]' " means nothing else than that which anything is conceived of as being in its own kind. From that comes the new word that we now use, derived from *esse*, the word for being: namely, 'essence [*essentia*],' or, as we usually say, 'substance [*substantia*]'; before these words were in use, however, the word 'nature [*natura*]' was used instead."[7] Simply by virtue of its continuity of being, such a nature, or *substantia*, was good; for evil could be defined as discontinuity, "passing away."[8] The fundamental axiom of all metaphysics, therefore, and one that Augustine cited repeatedly, was: "Every nature, as far as it is nature, is good."[9] Identifying in more detail wherein that "good" consisted, Augustine singled out three qualities, which he characterized as "generic goods": measure, form, and order. Where all three of these were present abundantly, a good thing was very good; where they were present only a little, it was only a small good; where they were not present at all, there was no nature, no being, and hence no good.[10] For through measure, form, and order, "existence implies continuance," and Augustine made his own the principle that "nothing is allowed in the providence of God to get to the point of non-existence."[11] Conversely, the presence of measure, form, or order even in things that were called "evil" was evidence of their continued participation in being; and "to recount such good things as these, and to speak of them as having no connection with God, the author of all good things, is to lose sight of the excellence of the order in things," whatever they were.[12]

For Augustine the Catholic theologian, however, this general philosophical question of nature or being took the specific form of the orthodox doctrine of creation. "Whatever is," as he formulated that doctrine, "must be either God or the creature."[13] In the ultimate and unambiguous sense of the verb "to be," of course, only God could be said to "be." The word to Moses from the burning bush, "I am that I am,"[14] implied that only God "truly is, because he is unchangeable. For every change makes what was not, to be; therefore [only] he truly is who is unchangeable."[15] God was, in an anticipation of the formulas of Anselm and Descartes, "the supreme good, and that than which nothing can be better, or can be conceived of as better."[16] Not to be God the Creator, but to be only a creature, was nevertheless a good: "If we were to say, 'Those things created out of nothing are not good things, but only God's nature is good,' we would be unjust to good things of great value."[17] But while the good that was God the Creator was self-contained and did not depend on anything else, the good that was the creature was good "by participation" in the supreme good that was God; conversely, it became "evil" by "falling away" from the supreme good that was God.[18] But then also, "the power even of those that are hurtful is from God alone," which included the very power of the devil, because God the Creator was the sole source of all being and of all power, regardless of the end, good or evil, to which it was applied.[19]

When applied to the continuity of human nature, this definition of being and creation meant that while "the whole of the world" in its infinite variety was a divine creation,[20] the human creature occupied a unique place. For, as Augustine went on to say, the human mind was also a creature of God— not more than a creature, as some wanted to make it in describing it as a part of God, but certainly not less.[21] The soul was to know, from the very moment of creation, that it was "not in its own power, but in subjection to God."[22] Rational and exalted though it was, therefore, the soul "was made by God as all other things that were made by God"; nevertheless, "among the things that God Almighty made, the principal place was given to the soul."[23] The rational soul had to come to terms with the reality of the doctrine of creation, which meant that it was "somewhat less than God, but only so far less that after him nothing else is above" it.[24] Therefore the rational soul and mind marked the human creature as having been made in the image of God. Rejecting the authority of the Old Testament as they did, the Manicheans did not regard as authoritative the account in its opening chapter of the creation of all things as "very good,"[25] nor specifically the declaration of that chapter that man was created in the image of God.[26] And when the apostle Paul spoke of "the new nature, which is being renewed in knowledge after the image of its Creator," they took this to mean that originally, as created, human nature "is not the image of God, nor formed by God,"[27] but that only the "new nature" of the new "inner man" as constituted and renewed by grace was entitled to that honor. Augustine rejected that Manichean distinction, arguing:

> *The apostle Paul certainly uses the expression "the inner man" for the spirit of the mind, and "the outer man"*

73

for the body and for this mortal life; but we nowhere find him making these two different men, but one, which is all made by God, both the inner and the outer. However, it is made in the image of God only as regards the inner, which, besides being immaterial, is rational.... God, then, did not make one man after His own image, and another man not after that image; but the one man, which includes both the inner and the outer, He made after His own image.[28]

Corrupted but not completely destroyed by the fall into sin, this image of God was the guarantee of the continuity between the state of nature and the state of grace.

Because it was conferred as the image of God the Creator, this continuity of human nature would perpetuate itself even in spite of human sin. "The question of the origin of evil [*unde malum*]" had been, according to Tertullian at the end of the second century, a continuing preoccupation of Gnostic heretics.[29] The very same question, in the very same words, was recurring in the Manichean vocabulary. "You Manicheans," Augustine charged, "often, if not in every case, ask those whom you try to bring over to your heresy, 'Whence is evil?'"[30] Otherwise they would ask it "as a last resort,"[31] but ask it they would. Augustine's response to this persistent question was based on a distinction between those human actions that could be ascribed to "nature" and were therefore necessary and determined, and those actions that were the result of "will" and were therefore free.[32] For the rationality of the image of God brought with it the freedom of the human will, and sin could not be attributed to human "nature," which was a creature of God and therefore good, but to the abuse of

74

free will. "Our voluntary sin," Augustine maintained against the Manicheans, "is the only thing that is called evil," and "the very possibility of the soul's sinning depends on free will." "I say," Augustine continued, "that it is not sin, if it be not committed by one's own will"; but "the soul ... accepted free choice, used free choice, as it willed."[33] All of this would come back to haunt him.

At one point in his controversy against the Manicheans, Augustine essayed to provide a definition of sin: "the will to retain and follow after what righteousness forbids, and from which it is free to abstain"; for "every mind reads, divinely written within itself, that sin cannot exist apart from will," and "if it is not free it is not will."[34] This was directed against the attribution of sin to "nature" rather than to "free will." Elsewhere, in his conflict with his Manichean debate opponent, Fortunatus, Augustine did speak of Adam as having "voluntarily sinned," as a result of which "we who have descended from his stock were plunged into necessity";[35] and, describing it as "most incomprehensible in its mystery," he pondered how "by God's most righteous laws, for the sin of old," the body had become "man's heaviest bond."[36] But in the course of making his argument against Manicheism, Augustine insisted that sin was a question of will rather than one of time,[37] and he ruled out of order an investigation into the historical origins of sin, which, he said, "befell human nature in Adam, of whom this is not the place to speak."[38] Eventually he would find "the place to speak" often and at length of Adam and human nature in Adam.

Whether or not Augustine thought it appropriate to speak about it, the continuity of the human race with Adam occupied a prominent place in Manichean thought, at least partly because of the means by which that continuity was accomplished: what Faustus the Manichean called "the humiliating process of ordinary generation, [in which] we spring from the heat of animal passion."[39] Augustine interpreted Manicheism as sharing with earlier forms of Gnosticism an intense revulsion at sexuality, indeed at the entire physical aspect of human life. He quoted them as asserting that "flesh is made up of pollution itself," and went on to describe in detail the physiological and dietary theories underlying their antiphysical, antisexual bias.[40] According to Augustine's reading (whether accurate or not), the antiphysical bias was rooted in the antisexual bias: "You dislike flesh," he charged, "because it springs from sexual intercourse."[41] On the basis of his Catholic doctrine of creation, he stressed that flesh as such was not pollution, for both the rational soul and the body belonged to human nature as constituted by its Creator.[42] Man was not the body alone, nor the soul alone, nor was the body of equal value with the soul; for the chief good of the body was not physical pleasure nor even physical well-being, but the well-being of the soul.[43] From this it followed that human sexuality was not to be equated with "pollution," but that if it expressed itself within holy matrimony, in what he called "conjugal chastity," it could be a means by which "those who are united are sanctified by each other."[44]

The practical expression of this Manichean revulsion at sex and the body was their cultivation of extreme forms of asceticism. Whatever may be the authority or the antiquity of the English proverb "Stuff a cold and starve a fever" (which, according to H. L. Mencken, is "not recorded before the XIX century"),[45] the contempt for the flesh as "pollution" and for the body as the devil's habitation has, historically, produced both methods of treatment, sometimes even in the same individuals or groups: a libertinism that strove to destroy the lust by a surfeit of self-indulgence and/or an asceticism that attempted by self-denial to starve the flesh into submission. According to its enemies, of course, it was always to libertinism and flagrant sexual excess that such a belief inevitably led, as we can see both from pagan critiques of early Christian worship and from early Christian critiques of the ceremonies practiced by various heresies, especially those we now denominate as Gnostic.[46]

In the light of this tendency in orthodox Christian polemics to interpret heretical assemblies as orgies of gluttony and lust, it is noteworthy that Augustine, who as a former adherent or "auditor" knew much about Manicheism although he had never been admitted into the innermost circle of the "elect," had to concede: "In your prayer meetings where I have been present I have seen nothing shameful take place."[47] Only rarely did he accuse the Manicheans of immorality, and then usually by repeating various bits of gossip about their conduct on the basis of what he himself claimed to have observed in their public conduct,[48] or on the basis of what "some are said to have confessed before a public tribunal, not only in Paphlagonia, but also in Gaul, as I heard in Rome from a certain Catholic Christian."[49] Most of the time he felt obliged instead to explain (or explain away) "their far-famed abstinence," as he had to call it in the very context of that gossip.[50] Rather than exposing it as a hypocritical cloak for immoral practices, therefore, he acknowledged their outward "chastity and notable abstinence," but interpreted it as a "trick for catching the unwary."[51] He admitted that "you do not eat flesh or drink wine," but he questioned their motivation for such self-denial.[52]

Above all, he contrasted Manichean asceticism and Catholic asceticism. Taking a leaf from the growing criticism of the excesses to which Catholic asceticism sometimes seemed to lead, he reminded his Manichean readers that "the abstinence and continence of the great saints of the Catholic Church has gone so far that some think it should be checked and recalled within the limits of humanity" (which is what Benedict of Nursia was to do a century later), adding that total self-denial of this kind "is beyond our tolerance, who can only admire and commend" such monastic athletes but not emulate them.[53] What differentiated a healthy Catholic asceticism from a morbid Manichean asceticism, in Augustine's judgment, was that "in the Catholic Church there are believers without number who do not use the world, and there are those who 'use it,' in the words of the apostle, 'as not using it.'" He concluded: "Why then do you reproach us by saying that men renewed in baptism ought no longer to beget children, or to possess fields, and houses and money? Paul allows it."[54] Catholic families and Catholic ascetic communities were both members in good standing of the one church, united in the bond of love; for "it is love that gives continuance."[55]

Ironically, it was from the ranks of the Catholic ascetic communities that there came the most formidable challenge to Augustine's dialectical theory of the continuity and discontinuity between nature and grace. "The monk Pelagius," as he was referred to,[56] took exception to a passage from the *Confessions* in which Augustine had prayed: "Give what thou commandest, and command what thou wilt."[57] This was too much for Pelagius to bear,[58] for it seemed to sever the moral nerve and to render the believer purely passive, contrary both to the explicit will of God and to the experience of all be-

lievers, and specifically of the 'spiritual athletes" who practiced the monastic life. Augustine reminded him that even
those who lived "in monastic solitude" had to pray, "Forgive
us our debts."[59] This is not the place to recount all the doctrinal issues raised in the Pelagian controversy.[60] Rather, the
controversy is of interest here because of its bearing on Augustine's understanding of the continuity and discontinuity
between nature and grace, as he had worked this out against
the Manicheans. Now that the Pelagians were attacking this
understanding as in fact Manichean rather than Catholic, Augustine endeavored to restate it against both.[61] With uncanny
skill, they identified as the five issues in their attack the very
questions with which Augustine had been dealing against the
Manicheans:

1. The praise of the creature
2. The praise of marriage
3. The praise of the law
4. The praise of free will; and
5. The praise of the saints[62]

1. "The praise of the creature" and thus the continuity of
creation had been the fundamental component of Augustine's
Catholic case against Manicheism. In making the case, he had,
as had been his wont,[63] assiduously avoided coming to any
definite conclusion on the touchy question of origin of the soul.
Whether, in the preservation of the continuity of the human
race, "new souls are created by [divine] inbreathing without
being propagated" at each new birth (creationism) or whether
they were transmitted from parent to child along with the
body (traducianism)—on all such questions, through most of
the controversy, he maintained a discreet skepticism.[64] The
key term in both the Manichean and the Pelagian controversy

was *nature* [*natura*], whose goodness as God's creation Augustine had been defending and whose sinfulness as man's condition he was now asserting. As has been noted earlier, *nature* was the standard philosophical term for what by the late Latin of Augustine's time was beginning to be called "essence" or "being." Unfortunately, that linguistic development could not undo earlier usage. "We were by nature children of wrath [*Eramus natura filii irae*]" was quoted by Fortunatus the Manichean against Augustine, who in turn explained it as saying that "anyone who is compelled by nature to do anything does not sin, but whoever sins sins by free will." [65] But Augustine was now quoting the same passage over and over in his treatises against the Pelagians, beginning with the very earliest one, written in 412. [66] When Coelestius posited a disjunction, Augustine's own anti-Manichean disjunction, [67] between "nature" and "will" and asked "whether sin comes from will or from necessity" and whether sin was "natural," Augustine replied by quoting this passage to prove that "sin is not natural, but nature—especially in that corrupt state from which we have become 'by nature children of wrath'—has too little determination of will to avoid sin." [68] "What [does the apostle mean by the words] 'by nature children of wrath'?" he asked later. "Was this the condition of the nature which was formed in Adam? God forbid! Inasmuch as his pure nature, however, was corrupted in him, it has continued in this condition by natural descent through all, and is still continuing." [69]

Clearly, the only way for Augustine to cope with the problem of the continuity of "nature" and with "the praise of creation" was to move from a formulation of it in categories of being or nature to a formulation in the categories of time:

nature as being *was* good now, as he had insisted against the Manicheans, because nature as being *had been* created good in the beginning and, despite the fall, remained God's good creature even now. Therefore the anti-Pelagian Augustine, no less than the anti-Manichean Augustine, was eloquent in singing "the praise of the creature" and of creation, but his praise (to resort to a pun that he himself liked to employ)[70] was sung in the tempo of time. For the Creator had also gone on to become the Savior, and it would not do to praise the Creator at the cost of the Savior.[71] This transposition of the doctrine of creation into the temporal modality is all the more intriguing in the light of Augustine's contention—for which he was criticized but not hereticized by Thomas Aquinas[72]— that creation was instantaneous rather than distributed over a period of seven literal days.[73] For as Thomas recognized, such a contention threatened to remove creation from time and history.

2. Augustine also made use of the technique of salvaging "the praise of the creature" by invoking the category of time when he was called upon to clarify "the praise of marriage" and of sexuality. Marriage was a divine institution (indeed, a sacrament of the church),[74] and as such deserving of praise. Augustine indignantly disavowed the contention "that we are condemning marriage and that divine procedure by which God creates human beings by means of [the sexual union] of men and women, inasmuch as we assert that those who are born of such a union contract original sin."[75] That was the dilemma in his interpretation of the continuity of the human race: to avoid Manicheism he must ascribe that continuity to God the Creator, but to avoid Pelagianism he must identify the union of man and woman, which was the divinely created means for

that continuity, as also the means by which original sin was transmitted. Once again, time and history came to his rescue in resolving that dilemma. In the commentary on Genesis that he was completing when the Pelagian controversy broke out, Augustine described in great detail what human life, including human sexuality, must have been like in the state of innocence before the fall. The words of Genesis, "And the man and his wife were both naked, and were not ashamed," meant that there was "no activity [*motus*] in their body of which to be ashamed."[76] Such would have been the self-control of Adam and Eve that their organs of sex would have been even more completely subject to their wills than our arms and legs are now, so that they would have been able to come together voluntarily and without lust.[77] But, Augustine added ruefully elsewhere, "how that could be, there is now no example to teach us."[78]

There was no such example of holiness, that is, but Christ the Second Adam. Augustine incorporated his "praise of creation" and "praise of marriage" into the sweep of history both by describing the sinlessness of Adam and Eve and by affirming the sinlessness of Jesus the Virgin's Son. Between them lay the continuity of the human race as a "mass of perdition which originated through the First Adam," but which could now be "justified freely in the blood of the Second Adam."[79] Continuity with the Second Adam could provide rescue from the consequences of continuity with the First Adam. But that continuity with Christ the Second Adam was, paradoxically, made possible by the discontinuity between Jesus Christ and other human beings: he alone had been able both to "undergo death of his own power" and "to be born of the ability of his mercy, not the demand of his nature."[80] With the exception of his mentor Ambrose,[81] Augustine was the first Christian theologian to develop into a full-scale causal nexus the relation between the sinlessness of Christ and the Virgin Birth of Christ, "who alone could be born in such a way as not to need to be reborn."[82] The marriage of Mary and Joseph was a genuine marriage, yet one in which through voluntary continence virginity was preserved.[83] On this "historical" basis Augustine felt that he was in a position, against the Pelagians no less than against the Manicheans,[84] to affirm a fully Catholic version of "the praise of marriage" by declaring that marriage was good but virginity even better.[85]

3. The very term "even the *old* law," employed by the Pelagians in their "praise of the law,"[86] had set this issue, too, into the context of time and history, for they had gone on in the same sentence to speak about "the prophets and patriarchs" of the Old Testament, that is, the Old Law. They had, moreover, introduced this praise of the law "in opposition to the Manicheans." Thus they represented themselves as standing, with the anti-Gnostic and anti-Marcionite church fathers of the first three centuries and (more important for their polemical case) with the anti-Manichean Augustine, in defense of the Old Testament and of continuity with it.[87] Like the word *nature*, the word *law* contained an ambiguity that was unavoidable but that could also sometimes be deliberate. "The true bride of Christ," Augustine had asserted against the Manicheans, "knows the difference between the letter and the spirit, or in other words, between law and grace"; for "the law apart from grace commands, but does not enable."[88] "We must distinguish," Augustine wrote elsewhere, "between law and grace. The law knows how to command, grace knows how to assist. The law would neither command if there were no will,

nor would grace assist if the will were sufficient."[89] But that distinction between law and grace was not, as the Manicheans supposed, identical with the distinction between the Old Testament and the New Testament.[90] Indeed, "the very term 'Old Testament' itself is constantly employed in two different ways: for the covenant with the people of Israel," which was how the Scriptures themselves used it; and for "all those Scriptures of the law and the prophets which were given previous to the Lord's incarnation and are embraced together by canonical authority under the name and title of 'Old Testament.' "[91]

When the Manicheans, in the name of the Pauline antithesis of "law" and "grace," had rejected the canonical authority of the "Old Testament" in this latter sense, Augustine issued his own "praise of the law" by affirming the continuity of the New Testament with the Old Testament. Now that "the praise of the law" had, however, become a means of demeaning the power of grace, it was essential to locate the Old Testament and then the New Testament—or, to put it completely, the New Testament and then the Old Testament and then the New Testament[92]—in the history of salvation. Augustine explicitly set this periodization of continuity in the history of salvation into antithesis with such a praise of the law: "We must not therefore," he declared, "divide the times, as Pelagius and his disciples do, who say that men first lived righteously by nature, then under the law, thirdly by grace."[93] This was equivalent to denying that Christ was the Savior of those who had lived under "nature," before the law, and of those who had lived under the "law," before Christ.[94] Thus the answer to those who rejected "the praise of the law" by rejecting the continuity with the Old Testament, as well as to those who affirmed "the praise of the law" by misreading the continuity with the Old Testament, was an interpretation of continuity and discontinuity that was cast in historical terms, on the basis of a sound "dividing of the times." And that, of course, was what Augustine was setting forth in the brief sketch of the "seven ages [*septem saecula*]" of human history with which he closed the last chapter of the last book of the *City of God*.[95]

4. When the Pelagian "praise of free will" took the form of an attack on Manicheism, this was in many ways a recognition of the most vulnerable component of Augustine's argument. He acknowledged as much when he charged that it was not against the Manicheans that they were maintaining free will, as rather against the Catholics that they were excessively extolling it.[96] For it was fundamental to his anti-Manichean case to maintain that sin, to be sin, had to be the consequence of the will, not of "nature." It was embarrassing enough for the Pelagians to remind Augustine about his earlier "praise of the creature" and of nature, but it was even more awkward to have them cast in his teeth his own "praise of free will." In the *Retractations* of 426/427, therefore, he was at pains to set the record straight precisely on this score. Thus in the treatise *On Two Souls, against the Manicheans*, he had declared that "sin is indeed nowhere but in the will," and he had defined "will [as] a movement of mind, no one compelling, either for not losing or for obtaining something."[97] "The Pelagians," he said wryly near the end of his life, "may think that this was said in their interest," and went on to try to explain it away. When writing against the Manichean denial of free will and their attribution of sin to "nature," he could not have anticipated that a few years later someone would come along, as Coelestius did, and draw the following conclusion: "Again the question arises how it is that man is unable to be

without sin—by his will, or by nature? If it is by nature, then it is not sin. But if it is by his will, then will can very easily be changed by will."[98] Augustine's *Confessions*, though written before this controversy, stand as the most dramatic refutation in Western literature—at least until Luther, Dostoevski, and Freud—of the optimistic belief that "will can very easily be changed by will."

That kind of optimism about the continuity of the will before and after grace was possible, Augustine argued, only if the human predicament were diagnosed as one chiefly of ignorance and of bad examples, to which the grace of Christ provided the antidote by instructing the free will. It was necessary to recognize, he insisted, "that free will, naturally assigned by the Creator to our rational soul, is a middle power [*media vis*], one that can either incline toward faith or turn toward unbelief."[99] Augustine's picture of Adam before the fall, therefore, described him as possessing not only a free will, but the superadded gift of divine grace. As a "middle power," free will could not by itself sustain him. "God did not will even him to be without his grace, which he left in his free will; because free will is sufficient for evil, but is too little for good, unless it is aided by Omnipotent Good," that is, by the grace of God.[100] By means of that distinction between free will as a "middle power" and the superadded gift of grace, Augustine sought to salvage the continuity of the free will before and after the fall while at the same time positing a radical discontinuity: before the fall Adam and Eve had free will and grace, but after the fall and by an act of their free will, they lost the grace, while still keeping free will, albeit in a weakened state because of the loss of the grace to sustain and direct it. Thus "there are both the gift of [the grace of] God and free will." [101] Augustine could claim that he, too, was praising free will and preserving its continuity even while exalting grace, because he made the relation between free will and grace a question of historical periodization.

5. When the Pelagians spoke of "the praise of the saints," they were referring, "in opposition to the Manicheans, who blaspheme the patriarchs and prophets," to "the prophets and apostles or saints, both under the gospel and in the ancient times [of the Old Testament], to whom God gives his testimony." [102] Augustine's response was based on his assertion, already referred to several times, that there was a fundamental continuity between the saints of the New Testament and those of the Old[103]—"whether they were found among the people of Israel themselves . . . ; or outside that people, as Job; or previous to that people, as Abraham and Noah": all had been saved by the same grace.[104] When the Psalms and the prophets boasted of righteousness, they were not referring to human achievement but to divine assistance, for they too would have to say with the apostle Paul, "Not that I have already obtained this or am already perfect." [105] The authentic praise of the saints was the praise of grace, and the continuity of the saints was in the continuity of that grace. Conversely, the continuity of the saints was in their sinfulness and in their acknowledgment of it.[106]

Were there any exceptions to this continuity, besides of course the totally sinless person of Jesus Christ himself, "who carried his humanity in the likeness of sinful flesh, without any sin whatever"? [107] In the midst of refuting, almost on a case by case basis, the claim that one or another saint of Old Testament or New had in fact been able to achieve a life free of sin, Augustine was confronted by the Pelagians with the case of the Virgin Mary, the mother of Jesus, and was obliged to reply: "We must except the Holy Virgin Mary, concerning whom I wish to raise no question when it touches the subject of sins, out of honor to the Lord; for from him we know what abundance of grace for overcoming sin in every particular was conferred upon her who had the merit to conceive and bear him who undoubtedly had no sin."[108] That sentence, coming as it did from the normative formulator of the doctrine of original sin, was to acquire a life of its own in late medieval debates over the immaculate conception of Mary.[109] In the context of this inquiry into continuity, its interest lies in the very exceptionality of the case of the Blessed Virgin within Augustine's version of "the praise of the saints": no one else among them— not even John the Baptist, who shared with her the position of providing the transition from the Old Testament to the New Testament[110]—deserved that praise on the basis of merit but only of grace, and even in her case the praise accorded to her was "out of honor to the Lord."

In his argument against Manicheism, Augustine had rejected its explanation of sin on the basis of a theory of "the antiquity of our times to which we return, and of our years,"[111] and he had not found it appropriate in that argument to pay central attention to the figure of Adam.[112] But as his thinking moved increasingly from Neoplatonism to a synthesis of the Neoplatonic and the biblical, and from the categories of being to a synthesis of being with the categories of time, he found the question of continuity and discontinuity inescapable and he responded to the challenge of Pelagianism by embedding both nature and grace, both free will and necessity, and even both being and becoming, in the all-comprehending schema of time and eternity—or, rather, of eternity and time. Every other question—even the very nature of the church—had to be dealt with within that schema.

VI ❧

THE CHURCH AS
TEMPORAL AND
ETERNAL ❧

IT MAY BE SAID," Van der Meer has observed, "that in all practical matters Augustine had a quite definite model before his eyes—his father in Christ, Ambrose."[1] For it was Ambrose the preacher who had converted him, Ambrose the scholar who had taught him how to read and interpret the Bible correctly, that is, allegorically, and above all Ambrose the bishop who had baptized him, "receiving me as a father would and welcoming my coming as a good bishop should."[2] And when, in 396, he himself became the bishop of Hippo Regius, Augustine stepped into a continuity not only with his predecessor there, Valerius, and with his episcopal father in Christ, Ambrose of Milan, but with the apostles and with all their successors in the episcopate, "the apostolic sees and the succession of bishops, spread abroad in an indisputably worldwide diffusion."[3] It was, as he had written while still a priest to bishop Valerius, a continuity for which his earlier experience as a professor of rhetoric had not prepared him.[4]

Yet it was not Augustine the professor of rhetoric, much less the professor of philosophy, but Augustine the bishop, who made history not only as a churchman, but as a writer and thinker. Even in a work presumably addressed to non-

Christians as well as Christians and dealing with many "secular" issues in history and politics, *The City of God*, he was conscious of speaking in the name of "the unity of the Catholic Church" whose continuity had come down from the apostles.[5] In both of the controversies discussed in the preceding chapter Augustine saw himself as cast in the role of defender of the continuity of the Catholic Church. Thus in an eloquent apostrophe to "the Catholic Church, most true mother of Christians," he invited the Manicheans to return to her bosom and to find discipline, peace, and truth in continuity with her teaching; and he appealed to the authority of what had been "spread far and wide for a length of time, and sanctioned by the concordant testimony of churches scattered over all the world."[6] And in his treatise *On the Proceedings of Pelagius* [*De gestis Pelagii*] he reported that Pelagius had affirmed, "I hold all things in accordance with the teaching of the Holy Catholic Church"; but while conceding that it was the duty of local bishops to deal with questions of morality and discipline within their own dioceses, he insisted that "impious doctrines put forth by persons of this character it is no doubt the duty of all Catholics, however remote their residence, to oppose and refute,"[7] thus appealing to the continuity of the Catholic Church in both space and time. Nevertheless, this particular continuity, in many ways so massive and (according to Augustine the bishop) historically verifiable, proved itself to be (also according to Augustine the bishop) highly problematical. For the church was both historical and eternal, and therefore its continuity as an institution was temporally palpable but its continuity as the company of the predestined was infinitely mysterious.

The institutional continuity of the church was grounded in

the office of the bishop: Augustine had believed that even before he himself had become a bishop,[8] and now he could make it his own. A few years after becoming bishop, he could recite the names of all the bishops of Rome:

The successor of Peter was Linus, and his successors in unbroken continuity were these: Clement {I, fl. c. 96}, Anacletus, Evaristus, Alexander {I}, Sixtus {I, c. 117–c. 127}, Telesphorus {c. 127–c. 137}, Iginus {Hyginus, c. 137–c. 140}, Anicetus {c. 154–c. 166}, Pius {I, actually the predecessor of Anicetus, c. 140–154}, Soter {c. 166– c. 175}, Eleutherius {175–189}, Victor {I, 189–198}, Zephirinus {Zephyrinus, 198–217}, Calixtus {Callistus I, 217–222}, Urban {I, 222–230}, Pontian {230–235}, Anterus {235–236}, Fabian {236–250}, Cornelius {251–253}, Lucius {I, 253–254}, Stephen {I, 254–257}, Xystus {Sixtus II, 257–258}, Dionysius {259–268}, Felix {I, 269–274}, Eutychianus {275–283}, Gaius {Caius, 283–296}, Marcellinus {296–304}, Marcellus {I, 308– 309}, Eusebius {310}, Miltiades {311–314}, Sylvester {I, 314–335}, Marcus {336}, Julius {I, 337–352}, Liberius {352–366}, Damasus {I, 366–384}, and Siri- cius {384–399}, whose successor is the present Bishop Anastasius {I, 399–401}.

"If the lineal succession of bishops is to be taken into account," he argued, "with how much more certainty and benefit to the church do we reckon back till we reach Peter himself, to whom, as bearing in a figure the whole church [*totius ecclesiae figuram gerenti*], the Lord said: 'Upon this rock I will build my church.'"[9] From Augustine's concrete actions, as docu- mented in his letters, it is evident that the continuity of the bishops of Rome in succession from Peter had endowed that see with special prestige and authority, so that it was appropriate for him to appeal to Rome, as "the apostolic see," in a disputed case involving him and other North African bishops, including "the holy senior bishop who was then primate of Numidia."[10]

Augustine's letters likewise provide evidence of the relation between a bishop and other clergy, both within and beyond his own diocese. In a class by themselves among these letters are the surviving sixteen epistles that he exchanged with Jerome—"a unique document in the Early Church. For it shows two highly-civilized men conducting with studied courtesy, a singularly rancorous correspondence."[11] As Augustine had to acknowledge, Jerome was unquestionably the greater scholar, a *vir trilinguis* as he was called because of his proficiency not only in Latin but in both Greek and Hebrew.[12] On the other hand, as Jerome had to acknowledge, Augustine was, also unquestionably, the greater thinker. But questions of ecclesiastical status and rank likewise played a role in this remarkable exchange of letters. Although the first letter of Augustine to Jerome has been lost, the first to survive shows him deferring to Jerome as a scholar but nevertheless greeting him in the salutation as "brother and fellow-presbyter."[13] But after Augustine's elevation to the rank of bishop, despite his continued use of the title "fellow-presbyter" for Jerome,[14] they were in fact not quite equals any more, and we find Jerome addressing him in the salutation of a letter dated 404 as "my lord truly holy" and in the conclusion of that letter as "my very dear friend, my son in years, my father in ecclesiastical dignity."[15] In addition to Ambrose, Augustine's model bishop was Cyprian of Carthage, a fellow North African and a martyr, who combined pastoral compassion with episcopal toughness; Augustine's *On Baptism*, written in about 400, consisted of a vindication of "the authority of the blessed martyr Cyprian"[16] against those who were endeavoring to cite him against Augustine.

Yet Augustine, like anyone who compiled episcopal lists, had to reckon with the possibility that "in the course of these centuries, through inadvertence," the succession of bishops might have been corrupted.[17] From the days of the early church, therefore, the guarantee of the continuity of the church by appeal to that succession did not stand in isolation, but was part of a more complex set of "criteria of apostolic continuity."[18] Another important component was the continuity of the tradition of orthodox doctrine as summarized in the creed. "We have the Catholic faith in the creed [*in symbolo*]," he said to a council of all the bishops of North Africa, "known to the faithful and committed to memory, contained in a form of expression as concise as has been rendered admissible by the circumstances of the case"; and then he proceeded to expound the creed, phrase by phrase.[19] Augustine's contemporary, Rufinus, wrote a more extensive commentary on the creed. Thereby he preserved the oldest Latin text of the complete Apostles' Creed that has survived, so that, in the words of his translator who is also a leading historian of early creeds, "the part played by Rufinus [in providing information about the creed] . . . cannot be exaggerated."[20] According to Rufinus, "the tradition of our forefathers" had described how, having received the gift of the Holy Spirit at Pentecost, the apostles of Christ, before setting out on their separate ways to preach the gospel to the world, were inspired to "draft this short summary of their future preaching" in the form of the *symbolum apostolicum,* or Apostles' Creed.[21] From Cyprian Augustine had learned "to go back to the source, that is, to apostolic tradition, and thence turn the channel of truth to our times,"[22] relying on the authority of this universal tradition.

Or, as Augustine put it elsewhere, in words that John Henry Newman said "kept ringing in my ears" as he pondered the claims of the Catholic tradition, because "they decided ecclesiastical questions on a simpler rule than that of Antiquity":[23] "*Securus judicat orbis terrarum,* The universal Church is, in its judgments, secure of truth."[24] Yet Augustine was to find, as indeed Newman would also find a millennium and a half later, that specifying these secure judgments of the universal church was not a simple task. For example, much of the explicit judgment of the fathers of the church seemed to emphasize free will at the expense of grace and thus to support Augustine's Pelagian opponents. To counter this argument, Augustine and his supporters appealed from the church fathers to the church fathers, viz., from the philosophical and theological arguments of the fathers to their devotional and liturgical practice; for what "the church has always prayed for" was what it had "always believed,"[25] even though the exigencies of its apologetic situation may have produced a different emphasis. And while Augustine used the authority and continuity of tradition as a means of explaining and amplifying the authority and continuity of the episcopate, he could also argue in the opposite direction. When the Manicheans laid claim to "the testimony from antiquity and tradition," he countered with "the testimony of the Catholic Church . . . supported by a succession of bishops from the original sees of the apostles to the present time."[26]

This doctrine of the reciprocity between the continuity of episcopal succession and the continuity of orthodox tradition sounds very much like a classic argument in a circle, defined by Aristotle as "circular and reciprocal proof . . . by means of the conclusion,"[27] a method of argumentation he attacks on the grounds that in demonstration "the same things cannot simultaneously be both prior and posterior to one another," but one must be a premise and another the conclusion.[28] A similar objection could be raised against Augustine's doctrine of the reciprocity between both of these criteria of apostolic continuity—episcopal succession and orthodox tradition—and the authority of Scripture. For when arguing against those who rejected the orthodox dogmatic tradition as articulated in the creed of the Council of Nicea, he appealed to the letter of Scripture, "the words of the Master," to prove the doctrine of the Trinity.[29] He likewise insisted upon the *ipsissima verba* of the text of Scripture when defending the integrity of the Catholic Church against those who charged that its continuity had been interrupted because its immoral bishops had fallen away from apostolic purity.[30] And he repeatedly disclaimed for himself or for any other Christian teacher after the apostles any authority on the same level with the unique authority of the apostles, from whom all subsequent teaching in the church was derived; for, he affirmed, "I owe unhesitating assent to nothing but the canonical Scriptures."[31]

Yet Augustine is also the source for a statement that was to become, in the Middle Ages and especially in the controversies of the Reformation period,[32] the standard formula for the reciprocity between the authority of Scripture and the authority of the church. For in repudiating the credibility of the Manicheans, he declared:

> *Perhaps you will read the Gospel to me, and will attempt to find there a testimony to Manicheus. But should you meet with a person not yet believing the Gospel, how would you reply to him were he to say, "I do not believe"? For my part, I should not believe the Gospel except as moved by the authority of the Catholic Church* [Ego vero Evangelio non crederem, nisi me Catholicae Ecclesiae commoveret auctoritas]. *So when those on whose authority I have consented to believe in the Gospel tell me not to believe in Manicheus, how can I but consent? Take your choice. . . . If you keep to the Gospel, I will keep to those who commanded me to believe the Gospel.*[33]

At the very least this meant that it was on the authority of the Catholic Church that the individual believer or bishop could discriminate between those books that belonged in the roster of the biblical canon and those that did not. Elsewhere Augustine could invoke a more nuanced method of discriminating between those books that were received by all Catholic churches and those that, while not received by all, had the sanction either of the majority or of the Catholic churches that carried the most weight, especially "such as have been thought worthy to be the seat of an apostle and to receive epistles" from an apostle; in the unlikely case that the majority of Catholic churches were to be on one side and the Catholic churches with the greatest apostolic authority on the other side in determining canonicity, it would be a standoff.[34] But from Augustine's own practice as a biblical interpreter it is clear that this authority of the Catholic Church in relation to the Gospel extended beyond the canon to the concrete questions of exegesis as well.[35] For after having discussed the way of determining canonicity, he went on to assert that if the precise meaning of a passage, even its pronunciation or punctuation, appeared to be uncertain, the reader was to "consult the rule of faith which he has gathered from the plainer passages of Scripture and from the authority of the church."[36]

In his use of these three "criteria of apostolic continuity"—the apostolic episcopate, the apostolic tradition, and the apostolic Scriptures—and even in the circularity of his method of arguing for each definition of continuity on the basis of the continuity that came from the other two, Augustine was himself manifesting his own continuity with the Christian centuries that had preceded him. As he replied indignantly to the accusation that in his doctrine of original sin he was still a closet Manichean, "My predecessor was Ambrose, who was not a Manichean. His predecessors were Hilary and Gregory. Their predecessors in turn were Cyprian and others too numerous to mention, none of whom were Manicheans. Nevertheless they taught the church what they had learned in the church [*Ecclesiam docuerunt, quod in ecclesia didicerunt*]."[37] Therefore Augustine devoted the first half of his speculative masterpiece, *On the Trinity*, to how "our predecessors" had handled "these and similar testimonies of the divine Scriptures,"[38] rehearsing, albeit without being able to suppress his own virtuosity completely, the continuity of the orthodox Catholic interpretation of most of the standard proof texts for the doctrine of the Trinity from both the Old Testament and the New. This he had come to know from his predecessors, chiefly from Hilary of Poitiers, who had the advantage of knowing very well the writings of the Greek trinitarian theologians.[39] Yet as the Augustine who was both orthodox trinitarian theologian and speculative thinker could not leave it at that but had to proceed to an exploration of natural and psychological analogies for the divine Trinity that would occupy the second half of *De Trinitate*, so the Augustine who was both Catholic bishop and speculative thinker had to posit a continuity of the church that was not only historical but eternal.

He did so even in the very course of defending the continuity and integrity of the institutional Catholic Church against the attacks of the Donatists. It was Augustine's concern in that defense to refute the historical charge that the infidelity and treason of some Catholic bishops in the era of the persecutions had vitiated the continuity of the Catholic Church, which was to be found now only in the faithful remnant of those who had separated themselves from Catholic continuity in order to preserve the true holiness of the true church. In addition to his other defenses, he also sometimes took recourse, in answering this historical attack, to the definition of the continuity of the church as eternal, not only historical. It was not just, he insisted, to base a judgment about the church on the state of the members of the church at any one moment in time, since "we see what they are today, but what they shall be tomorrow we do not know." That was, however, not how the church was viewed by the eternal God, "with whom the future is already present" and with whom consequently "they already are what they shall hereafter be." And so, "according to his foreknowledge, who knows whom he has foreordained before the foundation of the world to be made like to the image of his Son, many who are even openly outside and are called heretics are better than many good Catholics."[40]

Conversely, of course, others who were now evidently "good Catholics," who even held office in the institutional church, were, in the view of the all-knowing and predestinating God, not members of the true church at all, for God saw them as they would eventually and eternally be rather than as they were at one particular historical juncture. Or, as Augustine summarized a little later in the same treatise, "in that indescribable foreknowledge of God, many who seem to be outside are in reality inside, and many who seem to be inside are really outside."[41] Augustine recognized how this disjunction between the church as historical and the church as eternal could undercut the very life and structure of the institutional church. Each time he referred the continuity of the church to its eternal foundations in the eternal predestinating action of God, therefore, he immediately returned the basis of discussion to the criteria of human, historical judgment. While God predestined eternally, "we, on the basis of what each man is now, inquire whether today they are to be counted as members of that church which is called the one dove."[42]

The bearing of the doctrine of predestination on the relation between the historical and the eternal in the church became more crucial, and more ambiguous, as Augustine's predestinarian thought developed in the course of the Pelagian controversy. For in his works against the Donatists he was ever the Catholic bishop defending the continuity of the institutional church and invoking the definition of the church as "the number of the predestined" only when it seemed rhetorically appropriate to do so. But in his works against the Pelagians he was defending the very ideas of predestination and the grace of God, and hence the definition of the church as "the number of the predestined," even against what were presumed to be the presuppositions and implications of the institutional continuity of the church. When, for example, he spoke in one of the last of his anti-Pelagian works about church discipline and the practice of "that very penalty that is called condemnation [excommunication], which episcopal judgment inflicts, than which there is no greater punishment in the church"—a practice that his opponents charged would be useless if everything depended on the predestinating action of God rather than on the free choice of the human will—he found himself obliged, in the very same paragraph, to admit that "we do not know who belongs to the number of the predestined" and to seek to describe "the necessity of the pastoral office" as well as he could in the light of this circumstance.[43] Against the Pelagian claim that perfection was attainable under the conditions of historical existence, Augustine urged that when the New Testament spoke about the perfection of the church, this had to be interpreted under the categories of "distinct and appointed periods," of which the final "period," the eternal glory that came out of divine predestination, was the only one to which "perfection" applied.[44] Here in time the church prayed for forgiveness, but only in glory would the company of the elect be "without spot," as the New Testament described it.[45] "We call men elected" and members of the church if "we see that they lead pious lives," but in fact "they are truly what they are called if they continue" through the divine gift of perseverance; only those who stood in that eternal continuity truly belonged to the church.[46]

It would be very easy for such speculation to vitiate not only the moral admonition about which Augustine's Pelagian opponents seemed to be so concerned, but also the very structure and continuity of the institutional church: if everything depended on the absolute predestination of God, why bother at all with the church, with its episcopate or its sacraments? Recognizing this peril, Augustine emphasized that it was precisely as a bishop and in the name of the church that he was speaking against Pelagianism and defending predestination. Thus he addressed his *Treatise against Two Letters of the Pelagians* to Pope Boniface, to describe the problems that were "claiming [his] episcopal care and vigilance on behalf of the Lord's flock."[47] He insisted, moreover, that his emphasis on the sovereignty of the will of God in predestination did not turn the prayer of the church into a meaningless exercise.[48] He warned that it would be a mistake to preach about predestination, "whether to a few Christians or to the multitude of the church," without adding that "because no one can be certain of the eternal life" that was the gift of predestination, the members of the church were "to ask for it in your daily prayers."[49]

Sometimes he went beyond such practical reassurances to incorporate the continuity of the church and its sacraments into his theological interpretation of the total plan of divine predestination as well. For to avoid an "absolute vortex of confusion" about predestination and the church, anyone "who wishes to be a Catholic" was obliged to believe that God predestined not only ends but means: those whom God had elected to eternal life were also "predestinated for baptism."[50] For "between the beginning of faith and the perfection of perseverance there are those means whereby we live righteously; ... and all these things—namely, the beginning of faith and his other gifts even to the end—God foreknew that he would bestow on those whom he called."[51] The church was eternal because God promised and conferred the continuity of the church through predestination, but in so doing God worked through the historical church, its administration of the sacraments and its proclamation of the gospel. And, despite some of Augustine's occasional language distinguishing in the church between "the multitude of the called" and "the fewness of the elected,"[52] there were not two churches, one historical and the other eternal, but one single church that was both historical and eternal.

There were not two churches, but there were of course two cities, the *civitas Dei* and the *civitas terrena*, which were differentiated from each other precisely by the mystery of divine election.[53] In the very first book of his *City of God* Augustine reminded its citizens that "so long as she is a stranger in the world, the City of God has in her communion, and bound to her by the sacraments, some who shall not eternally dwell in the lot of the saints," while there were others "destined to be fellow-citizens" who now were numbered among its enemies.[54] As he pondered the mysterious continuity of the City of God, Augustine had to come to terms with the ways of a divine providence that had given power "to the Christian Constantine but also to the apostate Julian."[55] In such a context, a simpleminded equation of the eternal City of God with the historical and institutional church was impossible. Indeed, a careful reading will bring out the absence of such an equation throughout most of Augustine's treatise. After hundreds of pages about the City of God, there comes only in the twentieth book, as one scholar has said "suddenly and unexpectedly,"[56] the explicit identification of the church as the City of God. While still distinguishing even here between "the church as it now is" in history and "the church as it is destined to be" in eternity, Augustine nevertheless declared: "The church even now is the kingdom of Christ, and the kingdom of heaven." And he was at pains to specify that he was talking about the historical church, the institutional church, which was "now being governed" by the bishops and was now cele-brating the liturgy.[57] He did not, however, make clear whether he intended that identification to be retroactive to the inter-pretation of the term *City of God* in the first nineteen books, in which the continuity of the City of God within history and beyond history was grounded not in the institutional continuity of the hierarchical church but in the hidden ways of divine governance.

The distinction between the church as historical and the church as eternal was a way of putting the question of the continuity of the church into its larger theological and philo-sophical context. For when Augustine moves from his defense of the institutional church, its episcopate and tradition, to his description of the eternal church, known only to God in his predestinating will but nevertheless real and in fact the only "really real" church, it is unavoidable to hear the accents of his early and continuing Neoplatonism. Although, in *The City of God* and elsewhere, he conceded that there was in the thought of Plato "considerable agreement with the truth of our religion,"[58] and specifically singled out the *Republic* of "that demigod Plato" for praise because of its rejection of "the fictions of the poets,"[59] he did not, or at any rate did not fre-quently or explicitly, connect this *Civitas* with the *Politeia* described by Plato's *Republic*. Nevertheless, it is helpful to put our reading of *The City of God* into the framework of current scholarly disputes about Plato's political and philo-sophical intentions in the *Republic*. As Thomas Pangle has pointed out, "Even a superficial reading reveals that the *Re-public* does not deal much with political *practice*. Socrates never suggests that the regime articulated in speech be tested in deed, or that it be the direct guide for any program of political action"; and in corroboration Pangle quotes the statement of Socrates that " 'it makes no difference' whether the regime in speech exists or ever will exist."[60] Augustine's ideal City of God functioned in some of the ways that Plato's ideal Republic functioned, as a consideration of the eternal ground of justice and of love and hence as a critique of the historical attempts to embody justice and love in concrete communities and institutions.

Yet in most ways it is the contrast rather than the similarity between Augustine's *Civitas* and Plato's *Politeia* that is striking. Augustine spoke as he did about the continuity of the City of God because he was, in this very book, defending a concrete community and institution, the Catholic Church, against the accusation that it was responsible for destroying the continuity of the City of Man. Both Socrates and Jesus had been "calumniously impeached" by the officials of the City of Man,[61] Jesus even more unjustly than Socrates. But unlike the followers of Socrates, the disciples of Jesus had come back from the trauma of his death to form, in the name of his resurrection, a new community and a new City. Disciples had become apostles, and in continuity with them and their "successors"[62] there was, even now within history, the "one church which alone is called Catholic."[63] And ultimately—in the literal sense of the word *ultimately*, since the fulfillment and the fruition[64] would be only eschatological—this one church was both historical and eternal, in continuity with a Lord who was, as the church confessed, eternal in his origin and historical in his incarnation and now eternal in his reign.

VII &

THE CONTINUITY OF THE COMMUNIO SANCTORUM &

As a North African, Augustine had inherited an ecclesiology according to which continuity was significantly dependent upon sainthood, but by the time his intellectual development was completed he had transformed this into an ecclesiology according to which sainthood was dependent upon continuity.[1] His redefinition of the continuity of the *communio sanctorum* was to dominate—and complicate—the ecclesiology of Western Christendom throughout the Middle Ages and the era of the Reformation.[2] It would even figure in Graham Greene's profoundly moving novel of 1940 about a "whiskey priest," *The Power and the Glory.*

Believing themselves to be speaking as the faithful representatives of the continuity of the North African tradition, Augustine's Donatist opponents attacked the Catholic Church, and Catholic bishops like Augustine, for distorting the proper causal connection between the first two attributes of the church affirmed in the formula of the Nicene Creed, "and in one holy catholic and apostolic church [*et in unam sanctam catholicam et apostolicam ecclesiam*]." The first of these attributes, unity and continuity, was, they insisted, conditional on the second, holiness and sainthood. "By doing violence to what is holy," they charged, the Catholics had "cut away the bond of unity" and severed the continuity of the church.[3] And so, as Augustine acknowledged, "the question between us is, 'Where is the church?' "[4] Even more than other aspects of continuity, Augustine's definition of the continuity of the *communio sanctorum* itself had a continuity and a discontinuity of its own, without which neither the content nor the importance of his redefinition will be clear.

Augustine's own Latin text of the creed, as this is evidenced in his two expositions of it, did not include, after "holy catholic church," the phrase "*communio sanctorum,* the communion of saints,"[5] which is absent as well from the *Commentary on the Apostles' Creed* of Rufinus but does appear in the works of Nicetas of Remesiana, an older contemporary of Augustine, and in the so-called Creed of Jerome. There is, moreover, a dual tradition of interpreting the word *sanctorum* in *communio sanctorum* as either masculine ("saints") or neuter ("sacraments"), both of which are possible, grammatically as well as theologically.[6] Augustine often did make use of language very much like this phrase when he came to speak about the Catholic Church as both eternal and historical, as for example in one of the last of his commentaries on the Psalms:

"The Church of the saints" is the Catholic Church, the church of the saints is not the church of heretics. The church of the saints is that which God first prefigured before it was seen, and then set forth that it might be seen. The church of the saints was heretofore in writings, now it is in nations. Heretofore the church of the saints was only read of, now it is both read of and seen. When it was only read of, it was believed; now it is seen, and

is spoken against. The praise {of God} is in "the children
of the kingdom," that is, "the church of the saints."[7]

It would not appear to be doing violence to Augustine's thought and language, therefore, to speak about the continuity of the communion of saints.

As the appearance of such language specifically in a commentary on the Psalms suggests, an early and a continuing focus for this definition of continuity had been the relation of the Church to Judaism. The standard Christian reading of the ninth, tenth, and eleventh chapters of the Epistle to the Romans[8] indicates that one of the most pervasive ways of distinguishing between the continuity of "Israel according to the flesh" and that of "Israel according to the spirit" was to assert that in the latter the continuity was perpetuated not through membership in an external polity or institution but through genuine holiness. Thus "the oldest Christian apology against the Jews which is extant,"[9] the *Dialogue with Trypho* of Justin Martyr from the early decades of the second century, arrogated the title "people of God" for the Christians, and went on to explain: "But we are not only a people, but also a *holy* people. . . . [As the prophet Isaiah says], 'And they shall be called The holy people, the redeemed of the Lord.'"[10] Continuity was not to be sought in physical descent from Abraham; as Jesus himself had said, "I tell you, God is able from these stones to raise up children to Abraham."[11] Rather it was to be found in spiritual holiness and authentic sainthood.

Augustine's treatment of the relation between Christianity and Judaism furnishes striking evidence of many kinds that as, in his own words, "the church, which is the 'people of God,' is an ancient institution even in the pilgrimage of this life"[12] and had itself developed into an external polity, such a contrast between the old Israel and "the new Israel" had often become more difficult to draw with any credibility. In his treatise *On Lying*, for example, written just before his appointment as bishop, Augustine could speak of the priesthood of the old Israel at the time of the New Testament as "outwardly clean and fair, but inwardly foul with muddy lusts," as a result of which it was "ready to pass away through the vengeance of the Lord" and did pass away; and he said nothing about the question of the continuing efficacy of such a priesthood in spite of any inward corruption of the priests.[13] But now that it had become his responsibility as a Catholic bishop to defend the integrity of the priestly office—precisely as an integrity that persisted in spite of the inward corruption of the priests— he could treat the priesthood of the old Israel quite differently:

> *That a man should be a true priest, it is requisite that he should be clothed not with the sacrament alone, but with righteousness, as it is written, "Let thy priests be clothed with righteousness." But if a man be a priest by virtue of the sacrament alone, as was the high priest Caiphas, the persecutor of the one most true Priest, then even though he himself be not truthful, yet what he gives is true, if he gives not what is his own but what is God's; as it is said of Caiphas himself, "He did not say this of his own accord, but being high priest that year he prophesied."*[14]

And that, Augustine insisted, applied as much to the objective office of the Christian priest despite his own personal unfaithfulness as it had to the objective office of the high priest of

Israel: the continuity lay in the objective office, not in the subjective disposition of the priest or bishop, for what he conferred was true even when he himself was not. As proof, while the Donatists quoted the Book of Pslams to speak of the Catholic episcopate as "the seat of the scornful,"[15] Augustine repeatedly cited in support of "the apostolic seat" the statement of Jesus concerning the Israelitic structures of authority: "The scribes and the Pharisees sit on Moses' seat; so practice and observe whatever they tell you."[16] Augustine was, of course, still sure that the authority of the scribes and Pharisees and of the priesthood of the old Israel had been discontinued, but he did not attribute this discontinuation to the inner state of their hearts and lives, but to the coming of Christ as "the one most true Priest," who had superseded the priesthood of the old Israel and established the priesthood of the Catholic Church, which found its continuity in its succession from him and from his apostles.

As they sought to preserve and to enforce their standard of authentic holiness, the early Christians had, from the beginning, insisted on the practice of a rigorous church discipline. For the Book of Acts describes them as having "continued stedfastly in the apostles' doctrine and fellowship [*koinōnia*], and in breaking of bread, and in prayers."[17] It is evident from the use of the same Greek word in the rhetorical question of the apostle Paul (which Augustine's opponents were to quote against him)[18]—"Do not be mismated with unbelievers. For . . . what fellowship [*koinōnia*] has light with darkness?"—that this "fellowship" or "communion" with the apostles and the saints implied the enforcement of disciplinary standards. Sometimes, as in the case of Ananias and Sapphira,[19] it even entailed the imposition of capital punishment by divine intervention, since, in the chilling epigram of Jerome as he cited this incident to justify his own harshness, "there is no such thing as cruelty when it comes to regard for God's honor."[20] Probably the most austere formulation within the New Testament itself of this enforcement of disciplinary standards came in the declaration of the Epistle to the Hebrews: "For it is impossible to restore again to repentance those who have once been enlightened [i.e., baptized], who have tasted the heavenly gift, and have become partakers of the Holy Spirit, and have tasted the goodness of the word of God and the powers of the age to come, if they then commit apostasy, since they crucify the Son of God on their own account and hold him up to contempt."[21] Jerome took this to be a warning against "falling asleep when once we have been baptized."[22]

But to the North African moralist Tertullian, writing early in the third century and after his conversion to the even more intense moralism of the Montanist sect, these words of the Epistle to the Hebrews had meant that according to the standards of "the discipline of the apostles" there were certain sins—specifically, idolatry, adultery, and murder—that were, quite literally, unpardonable.[23] For the stringent disciplinary requirements of the Old Testament, far from having been relaxed by "the discipline of Christ," had now become more stringent still.[24] In voicing such "puritanical" views, Tertullian was in part giving expression to the idiosyncratic severity of his own personality: "Tertullian combines inexhaustible vigor, burning rhetoric, and biting satire. His attitude is uncompromising."[25] Yet his importance far transcends his own prejudices or quirks, for he was shaped by, and then himself went on to shape, the disciplinary rigorism of Christianity in North Africa as this was to be experienced by Christian leaders there until the time of Augustine and even beyond. As a leading scholar of North African Christianity has put it, "In his writings are to be found the main elements of the doctrine of the purity of the Church, of the necessity for 'rebaptism of heretics,' of martyrdom, and the moral austerity which the rigorists of later generations were to develop. Though we know not whether Tertullian had any direct influence on the Donatists, their thought was in many ways but a continuation of his own. It is perhaps hardly an exaggeration to account him less a Catholic apologist than the forerunner and father of Donatism."[26] "Direct influence" there may not have been, but there was a great deal of indirect influence through Tertullian's outstanding pupil, Cyprian of Carthage, the man who was the principal "support"[27] of the Donatists, and whom in turn, in Augustine's words, "our pious Mother [the Catholic] Church counts among the few rare men of surpassing excellence and grace."[28] Both Augustine the Catholic bishop and his Donatist opponents had laid claim to continuity with Cyprian.

Cyprian in turn affirmed a continuity with Tertullian. Our principal reliable source of biographical information about the early church informs us that "Cyprian was accustomed never to pass a day without reading Tertullian, and that he frequently said to [his secretary], 'Hand me the master [*Da magistrum*],' meaning by this, Tertullian."[29] Moreover, a careful study of Cyprian's commentary on the Lord's Prayer shows his "verbal debts" to that of Tertullian.[30] The same is true of other works of Cyprian as well. Cyprian also stood in continuity with Tertullian's moral rigorism, but unlike Tertullian he was a Catholic bishop and was therefore obliged to try to apply that rigorism to the concrete needs of the church of

Carthage and to do so under the pressure of the persecutions of the third century. The outcome of that obligation—or, more precisely, the outcomes of that obligation—accounted for Cyprian's ambiguous position as the spiritual ancestor both of Augustine and of his implacable Donatist opponents.

The development of Cyprian's views on discipline and penance can be traced in considerable detail from his extant writings.[31] In the aftermath of the persecution of the church under the emperor Decius in 250/251, Cyprian, who had been chosen bishop of Carthage in 248, was faced with the disciplinary and administrative problem of how to deal with those who, under pressure of persecution, had in one way or another compromised their Christian faith and were therefore to be identified as "the lapsed." Rejecting an easy reconciliation with the church as "a subtle evil, an innocent-seeming pestilence, which masquerades as compassion," Cyprian recited biblical strictures against trying to have communion simultaneously with idols and with the Lord, and demanded that those who had lapsed "make expiation for their sins."[32] But eventually he was obliged, out of pastoral concern and in exercise of episcopal authority, to "shut my eyes to many things, with the desire and wish to gather together the brotherhood."[33] The church was not, and could not be, composed only of saints. Where Cyprian did draw the line was at the integrity and moral purity of bishops and clergy. "We ought in the ordinations of priests," he prescribed, "to choose none but unstained and upright ministers, who, offering sacrifices to God in a holy and worthy manner, may be heard in their prayers." For, he warned, "the people must not flatter themselves that they can be free from the contagion of sin while being in communion with a priest who is a sinner."[34]

Augustine's Donatist opponents located themselves in continuity with that prescription of Cyprian. Communion with a priest who was a sinner would infect the church and the people with the contagion of sin. Moreover, it had done so when, in 312, the archdeacon Caecilian was elected bishop of Carthage and the bishops who consecrated him were suspected of having become "traitors [*traditores*]" to the Christian faith during the persecutions of the preceding decade by surrendering copies of the Bible or other sacred objects to the Roman authorities. As one of Caecilian's opponents put it,

> *In his Gospel the Lord says, "I am the true vine, and my Father is the vinedresser. Every branch of mine that bears no fruit, he takes away, and every branch that does bear fruit he prunes." Thus, unfruitful branches are to be cut off and cast aside. So, those who being in schism are ordained by* traditores *cannot remain within the church of God, unless they are reconciled through penance with wailing acknowledgment {of their fault}. Hence, no one ought to be in communion with Caecilian, who has been ordained by* traditores *in schism.*[35]

The Donatists charged that the North African Catholics who stood in continuity with Caecilian, and thus with the *traditores* who had consecrated him, had been "defiled" by that continuity,[36] and they chose Donatus to be their "true" bishop. Thus they were, in Augustine's opinion, defining the question of the holiness of the church, and consequently the question of the continuity of the church, as fundamentally a historical question, even though they sometimes based their accusation not on the Catholics' descent from *traditores* but on their imitation of them.[37] They claimed to be able to show that at least one of the bishops who had consecrated Caecilian had been a *traditor* in the persecution of 303 under Diocletian. From this historical evidence they felt able to conclude that with Caecilian there had taken place a fall of the Catholic Church from authentic holiness. That fall of the church had also entailed a loss of continuity; for, as Petilian the Donatist and Augustine in response to him were to quote over and over, literally dozens of times, "the conscience of him who gives in holiness [though these last two words were sometimes omitted][38] is what we look for to cleanse the conscience of the recipient" in the administration of baptism and in ordination by a bishop.[39] But the "conscience of the giver" had been polluted by the historical fall of the church. And the Catholic Church had been guilty of murder against Christ himself through the murder of his Donatist saints.[40] "Hemmed in by these offenses," therefore, Augustine or anyone like him "cannot be a true bishop."[41]

Augustine, the same Augustine who could spin out elaborate historical arguments throughout his *City of God* and could recite the list of bishops of Rome all the way from Peter to the present incumbent,[42] refused to allow the question of continuity, or the question of holiness, or even the question of tradition, to be reduced to what seemed to him to be a simpleminded historicism: "We do not ransack ancient archives, we do not bring to light the contents of time-honored libraries, we do not publish our proofs to distant lands; but we bring in, as arbiters betwixt us, all the proofs derived from our ancestors, we spread abroad the witness that cries aloud throughout the world."[43] The Donatists themselves could be "free of the pollution" of their ancestors, too, if they disapproved of their misdeeds.[44] Therefore he admitted that he "did not know whether Caecilian was ordained by men who had delivered up the sacred books"—did not know and, ultimately, did not care; for what Scripture told him about was not such historical trivia, but the Catholic Church as "the church spread abroad through the whole world, with which the faction of Donatus does not hold communion."[45]

That was the "communion" that mattered, and the continuity that he found decisive, a continuity no less Catholic in space than Catholic in time. Besides, whatever the validity of the historical accusation against Caecilian, it did not strike Augustine himself.[46] As far as he personally was concerned, he was able to declare: "I did not do what you assert: I did not deliver up the sacred books."[47] If "your fathers prove that our fathers were guilty of that sin," that simply meant that "they would not be our fathers" any more.[48] Otherwise, the Donatists were "persecuting our ancestors with false witness even now that they are dead."[49] And so Augustine rejected many of the Donatist accusations as gossip[50] and claimed to have substantial documentation for his own position,[51] as well as for his accusation against them as having supported the cause of Julian the Apostate and having committed other atrocities.[52] Nevertheless, he insisted that "even if we held no documents in support of our cause, or only such as were false, while you had possession of some genuine proofs of delivery of the sacred books," that would not matter. For the Donatists had cut themselves off from "the full and Catholic unity of the church already spread abroad and established throughout so many nations,"[53] beginning at Jerusalem and going out into the whole world and not merely "in the party of Donatus."[54] That true Catholic Church was "hidden from no one."[55]

To the Donatists' theory of guilt by historical association

and their consequent interpretation of the continuity of the communion of saints, Augustine opposed his own views of time and history and therefore also of continuity. He sought to shift the basis of argument from the alleged fall of the church in the past to the undeniable unity of the Catholic Church in the present,[56] although it was only through the course of history that this unity was now "in the process of fulfillment"[57] and only at the end of history, "the time of final winnowing," that it would be completely achieved.[58] In keeping with this view of time and history, he interpreted the words of Jesus about himself as the vine and his Father as the vinedresser, which the Donatists had quoted to support their accusation of a historical fall of the church,[59] to mean that until the harvest of the Last Judgment it was incumbent upon the true believer to observe Catholic unity and to preserve communion with the Catholic Church.[60] For "the church had not perished through a breach of its continuity, but was, on the contrary, holding its ground, and receiving increase in every nation."[61] Therefore, "inasmuch as the church continued to exist, it is clear that it could not be defiled."[62]

The crux of interpretation for this issue was the statement of the New Testament: "Husbands, love your wives, as Christ loved the church and gave himself up for her, that he might sanctify her, having cleansed her by the washing of water with the word, that he might present the church to himself in splendor, without spot or wrinkle or any such thing, that she might be holy and without blemish."[63] Like so many of the most profound theological statements of the New Testament,[64] this doctrinal description of the church came in support of a moral admonition, which seemed to imply that the doctrinal description, no less than the moral admonition, pertained to Christian faith and life here and now: as it was possible for husbands and wives to love each other here in this present life, so it was possible for the church to be "without spot or wrinkle" also in this present life. Augustine charged the Donatists not only with affirming that possibility, but with appropriating it for their own communion while denying it to the Catholic Church.[65]

Augustine quoted these words "without spot or wrinkle" from Ephesians at least ten times in his treatise *On Baptism, against the Donatists*, written in about 400;[66] but when he was writing his *Retractations* a quarter century later he felt obliged to explain that in these references he had not meant to attribute this quality to the church within human history, but only to describe its gradual movement in that direction.[67] In the interim, of course, he had become embroiled in the controversy with the Pelagians over the question of whether an individual could claim within human history to be "without spot," and he had adamantly denied this to be a historical possibility. And in the course of the Pelagian controversy he had occasion to draw a parallel between the two theories of historical perfection, quoting yet once again the words of Ephesians: "Pelagius was accused of having said: 'The church here [within history] is without spot or wrinkle.' It was on this very issue that the Donatists, too, were constantly in conflict with us at our conference. In their case, we used to lay special stress on the mixture of evil men with the good, like that of the chaff with the wheat, an idea to which we were led by the metaphor of the threshing floor. We might apply the same illustration in answer to our present opponents [the Pelagians]."[68] Neither the empirical holiness that the Donatists claimed nor the judgment of consciences that they demanded was possible "in this present world before the time," that is, before "the end of the world."[69] Until then, the church was a pilgrim church, still on the way through history to its goal.[70] Not one moment in that history, nor one local church, but the Catholic Church throughout time and space was the true church: "The field is the world—not only Africa. And the harvest is the end of the world—not the era of Donatus."[71]

Until the end of history, then, the pilgrim church would be a mixed body of good and evil, a threshing floor with both wheat and chaff, a flock in which the sacraments were often administered by wolves to wolves.[72] While insisting that church discipline must be practiced and was being practiced within the Catholic Church,[73] Augustine acknowledged that "everywhere, on both sides" there was a "multitude" of cases of clergy who had fallen into sin, so that "the churches are few and far between, whether in cities or in country districts, which do not contain men detected in crimes, and degraded from the ministry."[74] The difference between the two sides, then, was not in the empirical holiness of one or the other within history; neither side could win in that contest.[75] Rather, the difference was that the Catholic theory of continuity took account of the reality that the sacraments were often administered by evil men; for if a minister was a good man, he was a partner in the working of the gospel, but if he was an evil man, he did not cease to be a dispenser of the gospel.[76] Thus the church was indeed a congregation of saints, but one in which, "by the prayers of the saints who are spiritual within the church," the sacraments also of evil ministers were valid.[77] But for Donatist rigorism, the presence of evil ministers in the Catholic Church had disrupted its continuity; therefore, Augustine argued, the presence of evil ministers in the Donatist

Church would, by their own theory, disrupt their own continuity as well.[78] They followed Cyprian in his rigorism, but not in his adherence to Catholicity and unity.[79] Within such Catholicity there could be and were differences of opinion, but such differences did not destroy the unity and continuity of the church through time and space.[80]

The locus of that historical continuity was indeed a *communio sanctorum*, not in the sense of a "communion of saints" but of a "communion of sacraments," not the subjective holiness of bishops and priests but the objective "holiness of the sacraments."[81] "The baptism of Christ, consecrated by the words of the Gospel, is necessarily holy, however polluted and unclean its ministers may be, because its inherent sanctity cannot be polluted, and the divine excellence abides in the sacrament."[82] For that objective excellence and continuity, it was impossible to determine whether "the conscience of the one who gives in holiness" was holy and pure or not.[83] It was unknowable, but it was also "immaterial," whether the minister was a saint or a hypocrite—although for him personally, of course, it was not the least bit "immaterial."[84] The statement of the Gospel that "God does not listen to sinners" could not mean that the oil of chrism or the water of baptism administered by a sinner, even by a "murderer," was invalidated by his sin.[85] Such a minister administered a "lawful" sacrament, but he did not administer it "lawfully."[86] As this objective continuity through "the communion of the sacraments" was true now of baptism in both communions, whether Donatist or Catholic,[87] so it had to be true retroactively as well.[88] Historical continuity, then, did not lie in personal sainthood, but personal sainthood was dependent on the historical continuity of a church that was holy by virtue of Christ and of the Holy

Spirit who dwelt in it through the holiness of the sacraments.

There was one other line of argument by which Augustine, in his case against the Donatists, invoked history as a resource for affirming the continuity of the communion of saints. It belongs more to his political theory than to his philosophy or theology as such, and therefore it has been extensively studied by certain recent scholars, for whom the social history of fifth-century North Africa has been of greater interest than theology or philosophy as a way of understanding his life and thought. Viewed in that light, Augustine's formulation of Catholic continuity in response to the Donatist challenge must be interpreted also as an apologia for the state church, as supported by Roman imperial arms, against "outsiders." The basis of that apologia was in considerable measure historical. Augustine's Donatist adversary Petilian, for example, wrote a powerful indictment of the imperial church in the form of a commentary on the Beatitudes from the opening verses of the Sermon on the Mount, in which the blessedness of poverty, meekness, peacemaking, and enduring persecution, as praised and urged by Jesus there, was contrasted with the reliance of the Catholic Church on the military might of Caesar.[89] "What have you to do with the kings of this world," Petilian asked, "in whom Christianity has never found anything save envy towards her?"[90] In his sometimes rather embarrassed response, Augustine not only employed the rhetorical device known as *tu quoque*, reminding the Donatists of their alleged dealings with the emperor Julian the Apostate,[91] but he invoked the memory of the good kings of Israel, who had supported the church of that time, and then the memory of Constantine the Christian emperor.[92] What the Donatists were failing to recognize with this indiscriminate attack upon all kings, Augustine charged, was "the different character of the age"; they could not see "that everything comes in its own season," but instead kept on referring to kings and emperors who had persecuted the church in another age.[93] Eventually, however, "the order of events"[94] in the political history of the Roman empire had moved from persecution to recognition to acceptance to establishment, and it was essential to be aware of that order of events. Therefore "whosoever refuses to obey the laws of the emperors which are enacted against the truth of God, wins for himself a great reward; but whosoever refuses to obey the laws of the emperors which are enacted in behalf of truth, wins for himself great condemnation."[95] And now, in the case of the Donatists, "Christian kings are making decrees against you in defense of Catholic unity."[96] A polemical position appropriate to one stage of political history was no longer appropriate once a new stage had begun. The continuity did not lie in opposing all kings, nor did it lie in being persecuted: there could be martyrdom for an evil cause as well as for a holy one,[97] and a martyr's death could not sanctify or cleanse that. The continuity lay in unity with the Catholic Church, whether in persecution or in prosperity. As he sought if possible to do for himself, so also for this church Augustine wanted to appropriate the words of the apostle Paul: "I know how to be abased, and I know how to abound; in any and all circumstances I have learned the secret of facing plenty and hunger, abundance and want."[98] "Everything comes in its season," and for Augustine it was the secret of true wisdom—here and everywhere else—to recognize the times and the seasons.

VIII ↬

SIGN, EVENT,
AND SACRAMENT ↬

THE DISTINCTION between time and eternity, together with his definitions of memory and of history, provided Augustine with a conceptual apparatus for considering a wide variety of philosophical and theological issues, as these had been bequeathed to him from both his classical and his Christian heritage. Among these issues, none so strikingly illustrates the ambiguities of that dual heritage as the issue of symbolism— or, to put it in an almost unavoidable English alliteration, "symbol, sign, and sacrament." All three of those more or less synonymous terms appear (at any rate, in the standard English translation) within one sentence of Augustine's most important investigation of the issue, *On Christian Teaching* [*De doctrina christiana*]: "By the *sign* of the cross all Christian action is *symbolized*, viz., to do good works in Christ, to cling with constancy to him, to hope for heaven, and not to desecrate the *sacraments*."[1] But the cross was not only a symbol or only a sign or even only a sacrament for Augustine. It could be all of these because it had first been an event, "under Pontius Pilate" and therefore identifiable as having taken place at one particular historical moment;[2] only on that basis could it also be used "figuratively."[3] The relation of event to sign and sacrament may well be Augustine's most original contribution to what Ernst Cassirer, in the title of his most important work, called "the philosophy of symbolic forms."[4]

The thought of Augustine occupies a special place in the history of what has come to be called, though only in the twentieth century, the science of "semantics";[5] and whenever it is recognized that "semantics, too, has a past,"[6] that special place must receive attention. The problem of semantics was, in one form or another, to occupy him throughout most of his adult life, and even earlier. He tells us in the first book of the *Confessions* that already as a schoolboy his skill at manipulating words won him applause and recognition.[7] "It was," he acknowledges, "in eloquence that I was eager to be eminent."[8] That led him to a career as a professor of rhetoric, which even then he was eager to defend as a more serious intellectual pursuit than athletics or even drama.[9] Out of that seriousness about words and meaning there came his first book (now lost), *On the Beautiful and the Fitting* [*De pulchro et apto*].[10] From his later descriptions of it, this must have been an essay on aesthetics and rhetoric, and (if he is still alluding to it in his *City of God*) such semantic questions as the analogy between complementarity in language and complementarity in reality.[11]

Although *On the Beautiful and the Fitting* is no longer extant, we are fortunate in still having another early work of his, also mentioned in the *Confessions*,[12] *On the Teacher* [*De magistro*]. It was, according to Augustine's testimony in the *Confessions*, not simply his own literary composition, but was based on an actual dialogue that he held in 389 with his son Adeodatus, then fifteen years old, who died soon thereafter. His "talent was a source of awe" to his father. And well it might be, for in this dialogue the young man functions as far more than the "straight man" we sometimes seem to see in the Platonic dialogues.[13] Even allowing for a father's pride and a father's grief—there is some reason to believe that the book was written specifically in memory of Adeodatus—we can see in the delicate interplay of mind between father and son the elaboration of a joint inquiry by both of them into the problem of what a twentieth-century book of philosophy has called "the meaning of meaning."[14] And coming as it does only two years after Augustine's conversion and baptism, the exploration of "signs" in *On the Teacher* provides an introduction to the earliest stages of Augustine's thought on this question and to the relation of its classical and its Christian sources.

Much of the dialogue was concerned with the "complicated" business of how "to use words to treat of words."[15] "In all cases where words are employed and something is signified, we speak of signs universally and without qualification," Augustine asserted in response to his son's "hesitations" concerning the way we use words to speak about words; and "so every word is a sign, but every sign is not a word."[16] Gestures as addressed to the deaf or actions such as pointing must also be identified as "signs," even without words. Thus, as Adeodatus put it in summary, "a thing cannot be demonstrated without a sign, at any rate if the thing is an action in which we are engaged when we are questioned,"[17] even though it was possible to do so without using words as such. Therefore, as he said in a later summation, "it is evident that while sign [*signum*] signifies word [*verbum*] and vice versa, *signum* applies more widely than *verbum*."[18] Within that framework, it was accurate to say "that words are signs" and that "that alone can be a sign which signifies something"; but because such a word as "nothing [*nihil*] signifies simply what is not" and yet was both a word and a sign, a word of that kind could be said to signify not a reality, but "the state of a mind when it does not see an object, and discovers—or thinks it has discovered—nonentity."[19]

Later in the dialogue, addressing this fundamental question of the relation between sign and reality, Augustine proposed the thesis "that things signified are of greater importance than their signs," since "whatever exists on account of something else must necessarily be of less value than that on account of which it exists." To this Adeodatus provided the clever rejoinder that, for example, "the word filth [*caenum*] is, I think, far preferable to the thing it signifies,"[20] and that therefore it was superficial to assume that reality was automatically superior to sign. Here, too, some "state of the mind" was an inseparable component of the relation between sign and reality. The communication of the reality by means of the sign, consequently, must involve that inner realm of the mind, what could be called "the inner man" or "the secret place of the rational soul."[21] "The value of words" was, at best, to "bid us look for things," but not "to show [realities] to us so that we may know them."[22] In teaching his disciples the Lord's Prayer, therefore, Christ, according to Adeodatus, did not teach them words, but realities by means of words.[23] And that teaching of realities was internal:

Concerning universals of which we can have knowledge, we do not listen to anyone speaking and making sounds outside ourselves. We listen to Truth which presides over

our minds within us, though of course we may be bidden
to listen by someone using words. Our real teacher is he
who is so listened to, who is said to dwell in the inner
man, namely, Christ, that is, the unchangeable power
and eternal wisdom of God. To this wisdom every ra-
tional soul gives heed, but to each is given openly so
much as he is able to receive, according to his own good
or evil will.[24]

As that inner teacher, Christ was, according to the closing
paragraph of the dialogue, "our teacher who is in heaven."[25]

That juxtaposition of word and sign, sign and reality, so
redolent of the Neoplatonic doctrine of "recollection [*anam-*
nēsis]," as expounded for example in the fourth *Ennead* of
Plotinus,[26] appears to have left little or no room for the category of historical event—not by rejecting it but by simply
ignoring it. The teacher to whose word believers were to pay
attention was the Christ within us, "who presides over our
minds," or the Christ above us, "our teacher who is in heaven,"
but not the Christ behind us, whose life and teaching, death
and resurrection, at a particular point in history, were, for
Christian faith, the decisive *verbum*, the Logos incarnate. Augustine himself testified that the Neoplatonic books, not otherwise identified, upon which he came in his quest for wisdom
before his conversion to Catholic Christianity did teach him
the essence of the doctrine contained in the opening verse of
the Gospel of John: "In the beginning was the Word, and
the Word was with God, and the Word was God." What he
did not find there was the announcement "And the Word was
made flesh, and dwelt among us."[27] Or, to translate that report

into the language of our present inquiry, he had learned from the Neoplatonists about "word" and about "sign" and about "reality," but not about "event."

When, almost a decade after the dialogue *De magistro*, Augustine returned to the doctrine of signs in *On Christian Teaching* [*De doctrina christiana*], begun in 397, those same words of the Gospel of John served as the basis for a more sensitive and nuanced consideration. It was an echo of *De magistro* when he introduced the subject by saying that as the Wisdom and Logos of God, Christ had been "everywhere present to the inner eye when it is sound and clear." But immediately he went on to explain that Christ had now "condescended to make himself manifest to the outward eye of those whose inward sight is weak and dim."[28] The coming of Christ, announced in the verse of Saint John, "And the Word was made flesh, and dwelt among us," represented the perfect combination of word and sign, of sign and reality: "Just as when we speak, in order that what we have in our minds may enter through the ear into the mind of the hearer, the word which we have in our hearts becomes an outward sound and is called speech; and yet our thought does not lose itself in the sound, but remains complete in itself, and takes the form of speech without being modified in its own nature by the change: so the divine Word, though suffering no change of nature, yet became flesh, that he might dwell among us."[29] And that act of "dwelling among us" was a historical event, it was "outward" and not only "inward."

In *On Christian Teaching* (whose fourth and final book was not added until 426, nearly thirty years after the work had been begun), Augustine proceeded from his earlier fundamental distinction between "*res* [thing or reality]" and "*signum* [sign]": a *signum* pointed beyond itself to another *res*, while a *res*, strictly speaking, "signifies that which is never employed as a sign of something else."[30] Or, as he put it more completely later in the treatise, a sign was "a thing which, over and above the impression it makes on the senses, causes something else to come into the mind as a consequence of itself."[31] Signs, moreover, could be divided into "natural signs" and "conventional signs [*signa data*]"; for reasons that are not entirely clear, Augustine elected to deal only with the latter here.[32] These he went on to define as "those [signs] which living beings mutually exchange for the purpose of showing, as well as they can, the feelings of their mind, or their perceptions, or their thoughts."[33] Unlike "natural signs" (of which an angry face or tears would be prime examples within human life), "conventional signs [*signa data*]" (of which words were, of course, the prime examples, though by no means the only ones) were arbitrary results of an implicit social contract.

Thus the disyllabic word *lege* appeared in both Greek and Latin (and, although Augustine did not know it, in German, albeit with the first syllable lengthened), and in all three as an imperative. In Greek it meant "Speak!" but in Latin, as in the famous words "*Tolle, lege*" that Augustine heard in the garden at his conversion,[34] "Read!" (and in German "Lay it down!"): "All these signs affect the mind according to the arrangements of the community in which each person lives, and affect different people's minds differently, because these arrangements are different. Furthermore, people did not agree upon them as signs because they were already significant, but on the contrary they are now significant because people have agreed on them."[35] There was no inherent power to "make signs [*signi-ficare*]"[36] in these arbitrarily adopted signals; they were like the signals used by dancers, which had to be explained to the beginner.[37]

Unlike these "conventional signs" of language, "the science of numbers . . . was not created by man, but was discovered by investigation" after having been there all along.[38] As one scholar has put it, for Augustine "numbers . . . exist apart, a kind of galaxy in the mind's firmament."[39] Considered in pure abstraction, numbers manifested "fixed laws which were not made by man": the multiplication tables and the relation of odd and even numbers, for example, were not "in any man's power to determine at his pleasure."[40] There was no empirical basis for the notion of "one," which had to preexist in the mind in order for any multiples of "one" to be present there or in experience.[41] In the treatise *On the Trinity* Augustine took advantage of the number "three" in the creed to elaborate the theory that "six" was the perfect number, because "it is completed in its own parts" of one plus two plus three.[42] Again, the seven Beatitudes in the Sermon on the Mount multiplied by the seven petitions in the Lord's Prayer "comes out forty-nine," which, with the addition of one, made fifty, the number of Pentecost.[43] Seven was likewise a highly significant number, combining as it did the mystical numbers of three and four.[44] Thus Plato and Scripture were agreed that God had framed the world on numerical principles.[45] Augustine was quite willing to admit that he was following the lead of classical antiquity in his respect for mathematics.[46] But transferred from pure abstraction to practical application, "applied to the laws of figures, or of sounds, or of other motions,"[47] mathematics had a unique contribution to make—though not the supposed contribution being made by those who were known as *mathematici,* the astrologers.[48] For our purposes here, the principal element in the genuine contribution of mathematics was a "knowledge interwoven with time."[49]

For such a "knowledge interwoven with time" was indispensable to the proper interpretation of the "signs" contained in Holy Scripture, the principal purpose of the treatise *On Christian Teaching.* In the third book of the treatise Augustine took over and adapted seven principles of interpretation originally formulated by the Donatist Tyconius in his *Liber regularum* [*Book of Rules*].[50] The fifth of these bore the heading "*De temporibus* [Of times]"; despite that promising title, however, it seems to have confined itself to propounding a method "by which we can frequently discover or conjecture quantities of time which are not expressly mentioned in Scripture."[51] Tyconius's sixth rule, the rule of "recapitulation," came somewhat closer to articulating the pertinence of the question of time to the intelligent study of the Bible; for by "recapitulation" Tyconius was referring to the tendency of the biblical writers to "appear to be following the order of time, or the continuity of events," when in fact they were going back to earlier events that had been passed by in the preceding narrative.[52] Such insights enabled Augustine to explain away certain difficulties of biblical chronology, not only in the Old Testament,[53] but also in the Gospels.[54]

Yet biblical eschatology posed a far graver problem than did biblical chronology for determining how to handle biblical language about "time." For in instructions that belong to what twentieth-century biblical scholars, following Albert Schweitzer, have come to call an "interim ethic," the New Testament frequently seemed to make the shortness of time until the end of the world the ground for its moral imperatives. This way of speaking about "the last time" might seem to suggest that only "when our Lord shall have been revealed are men to give heed to these sayings," rather than doing so in the present. According to Augustine, however, such biblical language was a way of presenting what we have earlier called "the existential time-as-summons" as distinguished from "the historical time-as-sequence."[55] Therefore "the very time when the gospel is preached, up to the time that the Lord shall be revealed, is the day in which men ought to give heed to these sayings."[56] The biblical way of counting time meant that the experience of time-as-sequence, the very "passage of time," could become a means of learning the lesson of preferring eternity to time, since "while we live in time, we must abstain and fast from all joy in time, for the sake of that eternity in which we wish to live."[57] Time, Augustine sometimes seemed to be saying, was the *signum*, but eternity was the *res*.[58]

Because it was not with eternity as such, but with time and history that large parts of the Bible dealt, however, the biblical interpreter needed to come to terms with the obvious quality of Scripture as "a narrative of the past, a prophecy of the future, and a description of the present."[59] Transitory though it was as a means rather than an end for the pilgrim on the way to eternity, "the whole temporal dispensation for our salvation" was the form of language the Bible used to train its hearers here in time for their eternal destiny.[60] The distinction between *signum* and *res*, fundamental though it was, did not therefore do justice to the prominence that this biblical language assigned to historical events. The particularities of costume, of coinage, and of weights and measures were all arbitrary *signa*, invented by various peoples for social convenience, but with no intrinsic meaning of their own.[61] By contrast, "we are not to reckon among human institutions those things which people have handed down to us, not as arrangements of their own, but as the result of investigation into the occurrences of the past, and into the arrangements of God's providence."[62] It was characteristic of past history that it could not be changed, not even by historians, "because things that are past and gone and cannot be undone are to be reckoned as belonging to the course of time, of which God is the author and governor," and that was not a "human institution."[63]

A study of history contributed to the proper understanding of *res* and *signa* in biblical interpretation in yet another way, by enabling the interpreter to come to terms with the apparently immoral acts of the biblical saints, such as the polygamy of the patriarchs.[64] This was a topic that the Manicheans cited as proof for their contempt of the Old Testament.[65] But it was necessary in such historical narratives to "consider carefully what is suitable to times and places and persons,"[66] and then to take the narrative "not only in its historical and literal, but also in its figurative and prophetic sense."[67] At the same time, as Augustine warned also in the *City of God*,[68] these historical differences between various periods and between various peoples must not be invoked as a justification for moral relativism.[69]

Augustine's attention to the history of various periods and peoples, together with his deepening recognition of the central importance of "event" as a category of biblical thought and language, provided him with the means for breaking out of the simplistic two-level distinction between the eternal *res* and the temporal *signum*, and for incorporating *sacramentum* into the diagram of time and eternity. Denouncing as "a miserable slavery of the soul" the kind of literalism that "takes signs for things,"[70] he proceeded to a historical analysis of how that slavery to signs had worked itself out throughout history, both Jewish and Gentile. Although Judaism had sometimes been guilty of confusing the sign with the reality for which the sign stood, the signs of observance and the law in the Jewish tradition had, "for a season," focused attention on the worship of the one true God.[71] Paganism, by contrast, had worshiped its idols "as gods, or as signs and representations of gods," thus confusing sign not only with reality, but with unreality.[72] Judaism was a bondage to "useful signs," paganism a bondage to "useless signs"; but both were forms of bondage.[73]

Then he continued with his explanation of the relation between Christian "sacraments" and all such "signs":

> *But at the present time, after that the proof of our liberty has shone forth so clearly in the resurrection of our Lord, we are not oppressed with the heavy burden of attending even to those {Old Testament} signs which we now understand, but our Lord himself, and apostolic practice, have handed down to us a few rites in place of many, and these at once very easy to perform, most majestic in their significance, and most sacred in the observance; such, for example, as the sacrament of baptism, and the celebration of the body and blood of the Lord. And as soon as any one looks upon these observances he knows to what they refer, and so reveres them not in carnal bondage, but in spiritual freedom.*[74]

Thus the transition from "signs," whether "useless signs" as in paganism or "useful signs" as in Judaism, to "sacraments" had come through the "events" of the life, death, and resurrection of Christ. And those "sacraments" could be characterized as a special set of "signs" in which the "events" of the life of Christ were determinative.

Although Augustine, in the passage just quoted on the sacraments, referred specifically only to baptism and the Eucharist, it is clear from studies of his usage that in his writings he also applied the term *sacramentum* to other sacred actions than these two. He found it possible, for example, to describe both the creed and the Lord's Prayer as "sacraments."[75] With the ecclesiastical legislation determining that there were in fact seven sacraments, no more and no less (which did not come until quite late in the Middle Ages),[76] orthodox Western theologians strove valiantly to show that Augustine had in fact also taught seven, and the same seven, but they have found it extremely difficult to make that point stick. Thus, after reviewing a number of such efforts and doing his best to vindicate his master, one Augustinian was forced to acknowledge: "From these various interpretations the conclusion is evident [*iam colligitur*] that the Holy Doctor did not speak with sufficient precision" on this matter.[77]

One reason for the lack of precision was certainly the absence of overt controversy over many of the issues of sacramental theology. For where he was involved in such controversy, Augustine did find himself obliged to clarify his position; but in the absence of controversy he was able, with his "plenitude" of concepts and terms, to say both/and where later generations were to say either/or and thus, in the light of the precise definitions that they were to promulgate, to sound vague or even confused. In relation to those later definitions, it is of fundamental historical importance to recognize that of the seven sacred signs that were eventually to be identified by the medieval church as "sacraments"—baptism, Eucharist, penance, holy orders, confirmation, matrimony, and extreme unction—the only ones over which Augustine became embroiled in any significant conflict were baptism and holy orders. The objective validity of ordination despite the subjective state of the priest or bishop stood at the center of Augustine's disputes with the Donatists.[78] The sacramental objectivity of baptism, moreover, shared that position in the Donatist debates,[79] while in the Pelagian debates the necessity of baptism, and of infant baptism at that, provided Augustine with one of his most irrefutable arguments for the universality of original sin.[80]

As distinguished from the Eucharist, baptism (as well as ordination) was an action that took place once and for all in the life of the believer: Augustine insisted against the Donatists that even if it had been received at the hands of a heretical or schismatic priest, it was not to be repeated.[81] That made the "sacrament" of baptism an especially appropriate "sign" for the "event" of the death and resurrection of Christ, which had likewise happened once and for all, as the apostle Paul had vigorously argued: "Do you not know that all of us who have been baptized into Christ Jesus were baptized into his death? We were buried therefore with him by baptism into death, so that as Christ was raised from the dead by the glory of the Father, we too might walk in newness of life. . . . For we know that Christ being raised from the dead will never die again; death no longer has dominion over him. The death he died he died to sin, once for all, but the life he lives he lives to God."[82] To Augustine these words meant that while "in a mystical sense," those who lacked righteousness were called "dead," Christ would never die again; and so "they who are baptized by his baptism are not baptized by one who is dead."[83] These words meant, furthermore, that this "medicine" of grace as communicated through baptism was "mystically set forth in the passion and resurrection of Christ."[84]

Yet the very qualities of baptism that made it, as "sacrament," such a perfect "sign" of the "event" of the death and resurrection of Christ could become problems when Augustine came to the consideration of the Eucharist rather than of baptism. For although baptism, by being administered once and for all, represented the unique and unrepeatable death of Christ, once and for all, the Eucharist was, by the very terms of the institution of Christ, iterative: "This do, as often," he had commanded. Reflecting on this problem, Augustine wrote to his fellow bishop Boniface:

> *You know that in ordinary parlance we often say, when Easter is approaching, "Tomorrow or the day after is the Lord's passion," although he suffered so many years ago, and his passion was endured once for all time. . . . The event itself is said to take place on that day, because, although it really took place long before, it is on that day sacramentally celebrated. Was not Christ once for all offered up in his own person as a sacrifice? and yet, is he not likewise offered up in the sacrament as a sacrifice, not only in the special solemnities of Easter, but also daily among our congregations? . . . For if sacraments had not*

137

some points of real resemblance to the things of which they are the sacraments, they would not be sacraments at all.[85]

In that sense, Augustine felt able to conclude that "in a certain manner [*secundum quemdam modum*] the sacrament of Christ's body is Christ's body."

For in the case of baptism no one was in danger of supposing, on the basis of the words quoted earlier, that the death of Christ was being really and literally reenacted in the baptism of the believer: the believer did not die when he was baptized; besides, Christ had died by crucifixion, not by drowning. That was a classic instance of what Augustine in *De doctrina christiana* had described as a *figura*, which was not to be understood according to the letter but according to the spirit.[86] Perhaps the most fundamental method of identifying such a statement in Scripture as "figurative," according to Augustine, was when "it seems to enjoin a crime or vice, or to forbid an act of prudence or benevolence." And as the first illustration of this principle he quoted the words of Christ: "Unless you eat the flesh of the Son of man and drink his blood, you have no life in you."[87] "This seems to enjoin a crime or a vice," Augustine continued, and "it is therefore a *figura*, enjoining that we should have a share in the sufferings of our Lord, and that we should retain a sweet and profitable memory [*suaviter et utiliter recondendum in memoria*] of the fact that his flesh was wounded and crucified for us."[88] And in the event, when he himself took up the interpretation of those words of Christ, his language moved back and forth between real presence and figurative presence with such insouciance to the issues of the controversies which were to rage for a millennium after him that to this day scholars still cannot be sure just what he meant by some of his statements. The most celebrated such statement came in his question (which did not deal specifically with the Eucharist): "Why are you preparing your teeth and your stomach? Believe, and you have already eaten."[89] Eleven centuries later, the Swiss Reformers were still quoting this to prove that the medieval doctrine of the Eucharist had, by the doctrine of transubstantiation, lost continuity with the authentic Augustine.[90] Yet the same Augustine had, as we have seen, spoken of the sacrament of the Eucharist as a sacrifice of the body and blood of Christ, in continuity with the sacrifice on the cross. And it was specifically of the "event" of the cross, and specifically in his treatise about "signs," *On Christian Teaching [De doctrina christiana]*, that Augustine brought together various emphases that later generations would separate, symbol *and* sign *and* sacrament: "By the *sign* of the cross all Christian action is *symbolized*, viz., to do good works in Christ, to cling with constancy to him, to hope for heaven, and not to desecrate the *sacraments*."[91]

IX ❧

CONCLUSION:
CONTINUITY WITH
AUGUSTINE ❧

THERE HAS, quite literally, been no century of the sixteen centuries since the conversion of Augustine in which he has not been a major intellectual, spiritual, and cultural force. For more than a millennium and a half, continuity with the thought of Augustine has been one of the most persistent themes of Western intellectual history. Thus, although Alfred North Whitehead suggested in his Gifford Lectures that the history of Western thought could be read as a "series of footnotes to Plato,"[1] he could as well have said "a series of footnotes to Augustine." For during most of that history Plato has exerted his enormous influence not directly through his own writings, but through Neoplatonism, and this specifically in the form in which it was absorbed, recast, and transmitted by Augustine. In a history of Christian doctrine or of Christian thought, it is appropriate to recount that "series of footnotes" century by century, beginning with the Semi-Pelagian controversies of the century between Augustine's death in 430 and the Synod of Orange in 529 and continuing through the Middle Ages, the Renaissance and Reformation, and the modern period. For our purposes, however, it would be more appropriate to examine the theme of "continuity with Augustine" by reviewing some of the themes that have been engaging us here, selecting two that pertain to the generally philosophical or "secular" realm (Augustine's views of the self and of history) and two that belong to the specifically theological (Augustine's views of nature and grace and of the church).

There may be some controversy about the claim that "he was far and away the best—if not the very first—psychologist in the ancient world. . . . Augustine is an essential source for both contemporary depth psychology and existentialist philosophy."[2] But it is only necessary to read his *Confessions* in immediate conjunction with what is probably its nearest counterpart in Greek and Latin classical literature, the *Meditations* of Marcus Aurelius, to remark the fundamental uniqueness of Augustine's treatment of the self. Conversely, an examination of the continuity or afterlife of Augustine's book reinforces the impression of its towering significance for the history of the study and speculation about the relation between mind and will, between love and self-knowledge.

There were, of course, repeated attempts in medieval literature to imitate Augustine's *Confessions*, to write a sequel to it, or even to improve upon it. Perhaps the best known of these was the *Historia calamitatum* of Peter Abelard, of which Etienne Gilson has said: "It is no love story, but the tale of the incontinence of Abelard, victim of the noonday devil. But here let us pause and set it down to his credit that it is Abelard himself who furnishes us with all this damning information. He has his vanities and his failings, but he is no prevaricator. It is most unlikely that he is trying to deceive us. If it were merely a question of telling this story so as to exculpate himself from all blame, who could do it better than Abelard might have done?"[3] But in his "confessions" Abelard deals specifically only with the incidents surrounding his "calamities" with Heloise, and does not tell the entire story of a life. For an attempt to do that, we must turn to the *De vita sua*, written about 1115 by Guibert of Nogent.[4] Although it is, as an encyclopedia article has said, "a prime source for information about life in castle and monastery, educational conditions and methods, and most especially about the commune of Laon,"[5] it is inevitably disappointing to anyone who comes to it from an acquaintance with Augustine's *Confessions*. For while it may be permissible to call it, as its English translation does, an "autobiography,"[6] no one would think it accurate to rename it *Confessions*.

Indeed, both for that title itself and for the literary genre it represents, it is probably necessary to wait until after the Middle Ages, when Jean-Jacques Rousseau in 1772 completed his own *Confessions*, which Karl Barth has described as "an autobiography which had in common with Augustine's work of the same name an utter frankness and a very deliberate method of presentation,"[7] but which differed from Augustine's in fundamental ways. One other work deserves at least some mention in a discussion of continuity with the Augustine of the *Confessions*, and that is the *Secretum* [*My Secret*] of Petrarch, written in 1342–43. Its theme has been variously described, as Giulio Agusto Levi notes: "the modern desire for pleasure and for earthly happiness in search of self-justification"; "the vacillating faith, the weakness, and the internal contradictions of Petrarch"; and "a sincere document from the beginning of Petrarch's conversion and a proof of the profound influence exerted on him by Saint Augustine."[8] Significantly, each of these designations has also been applied to Augustine's *Con-*

fessions, and Petrarch seems to have been quite consciously relecting on the *Confessions* in this dialogue between himself and Augustine on the public reasons and private motivations that had impelled him to become a writer.[9] Indeed, whenever the nature of the self has become the object of investigation by the self, it has been almost inevitable that Augustine's *Confessions*, as the first and the most decisive such investigation (at least until Sigmund Freud's heroic self-analysis of 1897 and following), should continue to find an echo.

Much the same has been true of Augustine's *City of God*. The same editor and translator of Augustine quoted earlier on the significance of the *Confessions* for psychology has said of the *City of God*: "His view of the shape and process of human history has been more influential than any other single source in the development of the Western tradition which regards political order as inextricably involved in moral order"[10]—a judgment that would perhaps have to be qualified in the light of the influence that has been exerted by the fourth and fifth books of Aristotle's *Politics*, with their consideration of the bearing of "virtue [*aretē*]" on political order. Nevertheless, it is almost beyond doubt that for the use of the idea of design in history as a tool for describing "political order as inextricably involved in moral order" Western thought is fundamentally indebted to Augustine's *City of God*.

Charles Norris Cochrane, whose *Christianity and Classical Culture* remains one of the most provocative and influential accounts of Augustine's relation to Greek and Roman culture, came to that study fifteen years after an earlier monograph on Greek historiography.[11] From that background Cochrane felt entitled to declare that for classical historiography the conclusion was inescapable: "The process to which mankind is subject is therefore self-defeating; it is like the oscillation of a pendulum. To this truth point and emphasis are given by what Herodotus has to say with regard to the role of mind in the historic process. This role is simply that of a passive spectator, utterly without power to influence the course of events. . . . Subsequent efforts of classical historiography may be regarded as attempts to escape from the conclusions reached by Herodotus." [12] By contrast, he suggested, "to the Christians the failure of classical historiography was the result of its inability to discover the true "cause" of human being and motivation. . . . [Augustine] bears witness to the faith of Christians that, notwithstanding all appearances, human history does not consist of a series of repetitive patterns, but marks a sure, if unsteady, advance to an ultimate goal. As such, it has a beginning, a middle, and an end, *exortus, processus, et finis.*" [13] In articulating that view of history as a process of "a sure, if unsteady, advance to an ultimate goal," Augustine made the question of the pattern and meaning of history a part of the agenda of Western philosophy.

And so when Hegel undertook to interpret what he called "the course of the world's history," he based his discussion on an explicit echo of this Augustinian distinction: whereas "in nature there happens 'nothing new under the sun,'" it was "only in those changes which take place in the region of the spirit" that there could be genuine novelty and movement; therefore "the mutations which history presents have been long characterized in the general, as an advance to something better, more perfect." [14] Moreover, the concluding paragraph of Hegel's work reads as though it were a summary of Augustine's *City of God*: "That the history of the world, with all the changing scenes which its annals present, is this process of development and the realization of spirit—this is the true *Theodicaea*, the justification of God in history. Only *this* insight can reconcile spirit with the history of the world—*viz.*, that what has happened, and is happening every day, is not only not 'without God,' but is essentially His work."[15] When Friedrich Engels, commenting on the opening sentence of the *Communist Manifesto* of 1848, "The history of all hitherto existing society is the history of class struggles," declared that according to Karl Marx "the history of these class struggles forms a series of evolutions in which, nowadays, a stage has been reached" that would bring about the outcome of the purpose in history, he was describing Marx's effort not only, as he suggested, "to do for history what Darwin's theory has done for biology" but to do for history what Augustine's theory had done before him, only now not in the name of the City of God, but of the new classless society, which involved no less an act of faith than the earlier vision had.[16]

There is probably no concept in the Augustinian system that has been as pervasive in the history of Western Christian thought as his distinction between "nature" and "grace." Therefore continuity with that distinction has, more often than not, been taken for granted rather than argued by theologians. Although he did not invent it, he did give it the formulation that was to determine the continuity in later centuries. The uneasy balance between nature and grace in his thought meant that, like Augustine against the Manicheans, theologians could defend the integrity of "nature," creation, and human free will against its supposedly Christian detractors. Another possibility was to undergird the Augustinian balance between nature and grace more systematically than he had done and thus to "criticize Saint Augustine" in his practice by appealing to Saint Augustine in his principles.[17]

The first of those possible ways of achieving continuity with Augustine's theory of nature and grace is represented by Boethius. His *Consolation of Philosophy* was one of the most influential books of the Middle Ages.[18] Although there seems to have been relatively little anxiety among his medieval readers over it, modern students of the *Consolation* have been concerned about the lack of explicitly Christian references in the book: no mention of the name of Christ, no unambiguous quotations from the Bible, no explicitly Christian doctrine. Instead, it purports to give, through the mouth of Boethius's visitor in prison, Lady Philosophy, rational counsel about how to view his plight. Some literary scholars went so far as to separate the author of the *Consolation of Philosophy* from the Boethius who was known as the author of orthodox theological tractates used by medieval theologians, but classicists like E. K. Rand demonstrated by careful linguistic and literary analysis that the books were written by the same man. In his own book *On the Trinity* Boethius affirmed his continuity with Augustine, presenting "the seeds of reason from the writings of blessed Augustine."[19] Part of the solution of the puzzle of the *Consolation* would appear to lie in that same continuity with "the seeds of reason from the writings of blessed Augustine," which enabled Boethius, in the *Consolation*, to press the capacities of reason and nature to their very limits and, within those limits, to justify the ways of God *with* man and *to* man—not as though the grace of the incarnation and the cross were unnecessary, but as a way of showing that this grace was possible.

Medieval thought owed a great debt to Boethius, not only for his translations of the logical writings of Aristotle, but specifically for his formulation of the orthodox and Augustinian definition of "person," by which, as Gilson has said, "the whole of the Middle Ages is inspired and which has had such influence on the development of modern morality."[20] And the *Consolation of Philosophy* plays a decisive role in medieval thought and literature: it was translated into English by King Alfred, by Chaucer, and by Queen Elizabeth I; and it is present everywhere in Dante, who read it to console himself after the death of Beatrice,[21] and in whose *Divine Comedy*, it has been suggested, the words of Francesca in the fifth book of the *Inferno* about "*tuo dottore* [your teacher]" refer to Boethius in prison.[22] But it remained for Thomas Aquinas to put the *Consolation of Philosophy* into context by his reinterpretation of the Augustinian schema of nature and grace in the celebrated formula: "Grace does not abolish nature, but completes it."[23] Therefore nature was to be allowed to function as far as it could, but no further, and then grace was to complete it. That formula, unmistakably Augustinian in ancestry, enabled Thomas to formulate the balance between nature and grace, which Augustine had striven to achieve, more consistently than Augustine himself had often done, and thus to affirm continuity with Augustine on nature and grace.

On the other hand, the Protestant Reformers of the sixteenth century also claimed to be thoroughgoing "Augustinians" in their views of nature and grace, because, like Augustine against the Pelagians, they sought to glorify "grace," the sovereign will of God, and divine freedom against the supposedly Christian magnification of natural capacity. This they pitted not only against the medieval views of nature and grace, purportedly derived from Augustine, but against the medieval understanding of the church, for which Augustine was likewise the supreme authority. Therefore one twentieth-century exponent of Reformation theology has proposed the striking thesis that "the Reformation, inwardly considered, was just the ultimate triumph of Augustine's doctrine of grace over Augustine's doctrine of the church."[24]

Augustine's doctrine of the church as eternal and yet temporal, as spiritual and yet institutional, had enabled him to put the unity of the church, and communion with the church in that unity, in the position of the *summum bonum*, for whose sake he was willing to tolerate theological divergence and personal difference, but only so long as these remained under the single roof of the single house of God, the Catholic Church. Biblical theologian though he was, Augustine had likewise assigned to the church a normative position even in relation to the Gospel and the Bible.[25] And in his emphasis on the sacraments as the means of grace he had interpreted the hierarchical church, which administered those sacraments, as an institution of salvation apart from which there was no grace. In the hands of some of his medieval successors, that interpretation had taken a form that seemed to the Protestant Reformers to be threatening the sovereignty of divine grace by appearing to bind the action of God to church and sacrament instead of acknowledging the freedom of Spirit to blow "where it listeth";[26] for the very same chapter of the very same Gospel where those words appeared also declared three verses earlier: "Except a man be born of water and of the Spirit, he cannot enter into the kingdom of God."[27]

As Augustine's own exegesis of those verses demonstrates,[28] there was in his thought, and in much of the Catholic tradition, a fundamental tension between this doctrine of free grace or the free Spirit and this doctrine of the sacraments as means of grace. Although the thought of Luther both manifested the tension and strove to go beyond it, it was in the theology of Calvin that, in the words quoted earlier, "the ultimate triumph of Augustine's doctrine of grace over Augustine's doctrine of the church" took place. For Calvin took up Augustine's teaching that God could do as in his will he saw fit to do, electing whom he willed and rejecting whom he willed, and, by cutting that teaching loose from the equally Augustinian elevation of the sacraments as the primary means of grace, found his version of continuity with Augustine in the doctrines of sin and grace, election and predestination. "Augustine," Calvin asserted, "is completely on our side," and both in his *Institutes of the Christian Religion* and in his works of controversy he assiduously strove to refute the claims of his Roman Catholic opponents to be Augustinian.[29] Authentic continuity with Augustine lay in the doctrine of grace, not in the doctrine of the church; for the church, "mother of all the godly, with which we must keep unity" though it was also in Calvin's teaching,[30] was nevertheless the product of grace and the servant of grace, not its source or its sovereign. So it was that in the controversies of the Reformation era both sides described themselves as champions of the Augustinian cause, and it was only the radicals of the Reformation, and then some of the "reformers of the Reformation" in subsequent generations, who dared to dissociate themselves from that cause and to break with Augustine.

Just how important the continuity with Augustine has been for Western intellectual and theological history becomes evident from what an experimentalist would call a "control group," namely, that part of Christendom in which his authority has neither been continually affirmed nor even explicitly denied but largely ignored, the Greek, Syriac, and Slavic East. The earliest biography of Augustine tells us that some of his writings were translated into Greek during his own lifetime.[31] But those translations appear to have been lost, and only many centuries after his death, at the end of the thirteenth century, did Eastern readers gain access to a significant part of his works.[32] Many of the strengths and weaknesses of Eastern Christian thought can be interpreted as consequences of its not having had an Augustine. The only thinker among the Greek fathers who deserves to be ranked alongside Augustine for originality and genius is Origen of Alexandria, to whom a modern writer has applied the word François Mauriac originally coined about Pascal: "Every kind of greatness met in one man, and that man was a Christian."[33] But in the West, Jerome and Rufinus, Augustine's contemporaries, clashed over the question of Origen's orthodoxy, and in the East as well as in the West some of Origen's doctrines—though not, it would appear, Origen himself—came under the condemnation of the Second Council of Constantinople in 553.[34] Despite strong objections, especially to his speculations about double predestination, Augustine escaped such a fate, and went on to become chief among the fathers of the Latin West, a "Doctor of the Church."

He has retained that position through all the vicissitudes of Western intellectual and theological history. For example, it has been said of the dependence of Pope Gregory I on Augustine that "perhaps there has never been an author who owed more to the writings of another,"[35] and so it was to be throughout the Middle Ages. Even when, in the Carolingian period, those who espoused positions that they thought they had found in Augustine were condemned for them, Augustine himself escaped unscathed.[36] Augustine's theology and philosophy became a central issue of controversy after the introduction (or reintroduction) of the writings of Aristotle in the thirteenth century; but, as one medievalist reminds us, "it is against the evidence of history to range the thirteenth-century masters into two opposite groups: Augustinians and Aristotelians, as if they pledged themselves to follow exclusively either St. Augustine or Aristotle," when in fact "St. Augustine was the recognized Master of all, not of the so-called Augustinians alone."[37] As we have already noted, neither the Renaissance nor the Reformation presented itself as a challenge to that recognized position, but rather as a reinterpretation, or even as a reinforcement, of it. Moreover, the fundamental reorientation of Western philosophy associated with the name of Descartes was likewise a species of Augustinianism, and the Cartesian "Cogito ergo sum" stands in a direct succession, through the scholastics, with Augustine's use of thought and doubt as proof for the reality of the self and ultimately for the reality of God.[38] As one scholar has put it, "Augustine is the only church father who even today remains an intellectual power";[39] and so long as our civilization maintains its identity, continuity with him will probably always be characteristic of it.

ABBREVIATIONS
NOTES
BIBLIOGRAPHY ൠ

ABBREVIATIONS ॐ

My quotations from Augustine's works are based ultimately on the Latin text, but I have felt free to adopt—and to adapt—existing translations, without identifying them individually.

Acad.	*Against the Academics*
Anim.	*On the Soul and Its Origin* [*De anima et eius origine*]
Bapt.	*On Baptism against the Donatists*
Bon. conjug.	*On the Good of Marriage* [*De bono conjugali*]
Cat. rud.	*On Catechizing Children* [*De catechizandis rudibus*]
Civ.	*City of God* [*De civitate Dei*]
Conf.	*Confessions*
Cons. ev.	*On the Consensus of the Evangelists*
Corrept.	*On Rebuke and Grace* [*De correptione et gratia*]
Doct. christ.	*On Christian Teaching* [*De doctrina christiana*]
Duab. anim.	*On Two Souls against the Manicheans* [*De duabus animabus contra Manicheos*]
Enchir.	*Enchiridion*
Ep.	*Epistles*
Ep. fund.	*Against the Epistle of Manicheus Called Fundamental*

Ep. Joh.	*Exposition of the First Epistle of John*
Ev. Joh.	*Exposition of the Gospel of John*
Faust.	*Against Faustus the Manichean*
Fid. symb.	*On Faith and the Creed [De fide et symbolo]*
Fort.	*Disputation against Fortunatus*
Gen. litt.	*Exposition of Genesis according to the Letter [De Genesi ad litteram}*
Gest. Pelag.	*On the Proceedings of Pelagius [De gestis Pelagii]*
Grat.	*On Grace [De gratia]*
Jul. op. imperf.	*Incomplete Work against Julian [Contra secundam Juliani responsionem opus imperfectum]*
Lib. arb.	*On Free Will [De libero arbitrio]*
Mag.	*On the Teacher [De magistro]*
Mend.	*On Lying [De mendacio]*
Mor. Cath.	*On the Morals of the Catholic Church*
Mor. Manich.	*On the Morals of the Manicheans*
Nat. bon.	*On the Nature of the Good against the Manicheans [De natura boni contra Manicheos]*
Nat. grat.	*On Nature and Grace [De natura et gratia]*
Nupt. concup.	*On Marriage and Concupiscence [De nuptiis et conscupiscentia]*
Parm.	*Against the Epistle of Parmenianus*
Pecc. merit.	*On the Merits and the Remission of Sins [De peccatorum meritis et remissione]*
Pecc. orig.	*On Original Sin [De peccato originali]*
Pelag.	*Against Two Epistles of the Pelagians*
Perf. just.	*On Man's Perfection in Righteousness [De perfectione justitiae hominis]*
Persev.	*On the Gift of Perseverance*
Petil.	*Against the Letters of Petilian*

Praed. sanct.	On the Predestination of the Saints [De praedestinatione sanctorum]
Ps.	Exposition of the Psalms
Retract.	Retractations
Serm.	Sermons
Serm. mont.	Our Lord's Sermon on the Mount [De sermone Domini in monte]
Soliloq.	Soliloquies
Spir. litt.	On the Spirit and the Letter [De spiritu et littera]
Symb.	On the Creed to Catechumens [De symbolo ad catechumenos]
Trin.	On the Trinity

NOTES ❧

I. INTRODUCTION: CONVERSION AND CONTINUITY

1. Eusebius *Life of Constantine* 1.28.

2. *Conf.* 3.4.7; *Fid. symb.* 3.3.

3. Eusebius *Ecclesiastical History* 9.9.10–11.

4. *Mor. Man.* 6.8.

5. Etienne Gilson, *Reason and Revelation in the Middle Ages* (New York, 1938), pp. 17, 20.

6. *Trin.* 5.1.2.

7. *Ep. fund.* 14.17.

8. *Trin.* 1.4.7.

9. Peter Brown, "The Diffusion of Manichaeism in the Roman Empire," *Journal of Roman Studies* 59 (1969):92–103.

10. Frederick Cornwallis Conybeare, "Manichaeism," *Encyclopaedia Britannica*, 11th ed.

11. *Conf.* 5.5.9.

12. *Conf.* 3.6.10.

13. *Faust.* 11.2.

14. *Fort.* 1.

15. *Mor. Cath.* 30.62; 34.76.

16. *Mor. Cath.* 17.32.

17. *Faust.* 16.20.

18. That is evident from his comment, *Mor. Cath.* 1.1.

19. *Faust.* 16.1.

20. Ap. *Faust.* 16.7.

21. *Faust.* 16.20.

22. See Bernhard Blumenkranz, *Die Judenpredigt Augustins: Ein Beitrag zur Geschichte der jüdisch-christlichen Beziehungen in den ersten Jahrhunderten* (Basel, 1946) for a careful and perceptive evaluation.

23. *Mor. Cath.* 17.30.

24. *Faust.* 32.9.

25. Hilary *On the Trinity* 10.40.

26. Hilary *On the Trinity* 11.17.

27. *Conf.* 1.14.23.

28. Peter Brown, *Augustine of Hippo,* pp. 36, 273.

29. *Conf.* 7.9.13.

30. See, for example, *Ep. fund.* 39.45.

31. *Ep.* 28.2.2.

32. *Praed. sanct.* 14.27.

33. *Gest. Pelag.* 1.1–2.

34. *Praed. sanct.* 14.27.

35. G. L. Prestige, *God in Patristic Thought* (London, 1956), pp. x–xi.

36. *Trin.* 5.8.10.

37. See also pp. 62–63 below.

38. *Conf.* 4.2.2.

39. *Conf.* 5.6.10.

40. *Conf.* 5.14.24.

41. Brown, *Augustine of Hippo,* p. 256.

42. *Doct. christ.* 4.7.21.

43. George A. Kennedy, *Greek Rhetoric under Christian Emperors* (Princeton, 1983), pp. 182–83.

44. *Fort.* 19.

45. *Fort.* 13; 25.

46. *Fort.* 17.

47. *Ep. fund.* 14.17.

48. It will be a fundamental source for the discussion of Augustine's theory of signs in chap. 8.

49. *Doct. christ.* 4.2.3.

50. *Doct. christ.* 4.3.4.

51. *Doct. christ.* 4.12.27–28.

52. *Doct. christ.* 4.13.29.

53. *Conf.* 7.9.13.

54. See Paul Henry, *Plotin et l'Occident* (Louvain, 1934), pp. 44–62.

55. *Conf.* 7.10.16.

56. *Conf.* 7.9.13–14.

57. *Mag.* 11.38; see also pp. 124–28 below.

58. *Retract.* 1.1.4.

59. *Acad.* 3.20.43.

60. Possidius *Life of Augustine* 28.

II. THE CONTINUITY OF THE SELF

1. *Soliloq.* 1.2.7.

2. *Conf.* 10.8.15

3. *Conf.* 10.33.50.

4. *Conf.* 1.5.6.

5. Petrarch, "The Ascent of Mount Ventoux," *The Renaissance Philosophy of Man,* ed. Ernst Cassirer et al. (Chicago, 1948), p. 44 (see also pp. 141–42 below); *Conf.* 10.8.15.

6. *Conf.* 13.21.30; *Trin.* 12.10.15; *Trin.* pr. 1.

7. *Conf.* 10.23.34.

8. *Conf.* 10.32.48.

9. *Conf.* 1.6.10.

10. *Conf.* 1.7.12.

11. *Conf.* 1.7.11.

12. *Trin.* 13.10.25.

13. *Trin.* 8.6.9.

14. Vergil *Aeneid* 3.629; *Trin.* 14.11.14.

15. Etienne Gilson, *L'esprit de la philosophie médiévale,* 2d ed. (Paris, 1944), pp. 214–33.

16. *Conf.* 7.10.16.

17. *Civ.* 11.28 (Luke 18:17).

18. *Conf.* 1.19.31.

19. *Trin.* 14.14.18.

20. *Conf.* 10.21.30; 10.8.12; 10.8.16; 10.12.19.

21. *Conf.* 10.25.36.
22. *Conf.* 1.12–13.
23. *Conf.* 1.12.21; 10.34.41.
24. *Trin.* 11.10.17; Juvenal *Satires* 6.165.
25. *Trin.* 9.11.16.
26. *Conf.* 10.8.12; *Trin.* 15.12.22; *Conf.* 10.40.65.
27. *Conf.* 10.8.12–13.
28. *Conf.* 10.9.16–17; *Doct. christ.* 2.1.2 (see also pp. 128–29 below).
29. *Conf.* 10.11.18; *Trin.* 14.10.13.
30. *Trin.* 14.7.10.
31. *Civ.* 19.3.
32. *Trin.* 15.15.24.
33. *Trin.* 15.21.40.
34. *Conf.* 10.8.15.
35. *Trin.* 10.8.11.
36. *Trin.* 15.15.25.
37. *Trin.* 11.8.15.
38. *Ep. fund.* 17.20.; *Trin.* 12.2.2.
39. *Trin.* 11.10.17.
40. *Trin.* 14.6.8.
41. *Conf.* 10.8.14.
42. *Conf.* 6.11.18.
43. *Conf.* 10.13.20.
44. *Conf.* 10.15.23.
45. *Conf.* 1.6.9.
46. *Conf.* 1.19.31.
47. *Trin.* 14.5.7.
48. *Conf.* 1.8.13.
49. *Conf.* 10.14.21.
50. *Conf.* 9.9.22.
51. *Conf.* 9.12.33.
52. *Conf.* 1.11.17; 2.3.8.

53. *Conf.* 6.13.23; 3.11.21.
54. *Conf.* 5.7.12; 5.8.15; 5.9.17; and Augustine's own tears, 8.12.28.
55. *Conf.* 9.8.17.
56. *Conf.* 1.7.12.
57. *Trin.* 10.10.13.
58. *Conf.* 10.16.24.
59. *Conf.* 10.19.28.
60. *Conf.* 10.11.18.
61. *Trin.* 9.6.10–7.12.
62. *Conf.* 10.12.19.
63. *Trin.* 9.6.9.
64. *Conf.* 10.10.17; see *Trin.* 12.14.23.
65. See pp. 126–27 below.
66. *Trin.* 12.15.24.
67. *Conf.* 10.26.37.
68. Albert C. Outler, Introduction, p. 17.
69. *Conf.* 2.7.15.
70. *Conf.* 4.1.1.
71. *Conf.* 10.30.41.
72. *Conf.* 9.4.9; 9.7.16.
73. *Conf.* 5.1.1.; 2.3.5.
74. *Conf.* 4.1.1.
75. *Conf.* 11.2.2; 10.6.8; *Civ.* 19.17.
76. *Conf.* 11.18.23.
77. *Conf.* 11.14.17.
78. *Conf.* 13.11.
79. *Conf.* 11.20.26.
80. *Conf.* 11.27.34–35; *Ep. fund.* 41.47.
81. *Conf.* 11.27.36.
82. *Conf.* 11.28.37.
83. *Conf.* 7.17.23; 9.10.24.
84. *Conf.* 12.29.40.

85. *Civ.* 18.3.
86. *Conf.* 12.8.8.
87. *Conf.* 11.23.30; 11.21.28.
88. *Conf.* 11.15.18–20.
89. *Conf.* 11.26.33.
90. *Conf.* 11.27.35–36.
91. *Conf.* 12.11.13; 13.18.22; 8.1.1.
92. *Civ.* 11.6; *Conf.* 11.30.40.
93. *Conf.* 11.4.6; 12.8.8.
94. *Conf.* 7.11.17.
95. *Trin.* 13.1.2.
96. *Conf.* 7.5.7.
97. *Trin.* 12.14.22.
98. *Pecc. merit.* 1.2.2; *Civ.* 10.31; *Trin.* 2.9.15.
99. *Civ.* 22.1.
100. *Nat. bon.* 1.1.
101. *Conf.* 7.5.7.
102. *Civ.* 12.3.
103. *Civ.* 14.5.
104. *Civ.* 15.22.
105. *Civ.* 12.8.
106. *Civ.* 12.6; 8.25.
107. *Civ.* 10.22.
108. *Conf.* 4.5.10; Ovid *Remedium amoris* 131.
109. *Conf.* 4.8.13.
110. *Conf.* 7.1.1.
111. *Trin.* 14.1.3.
112. *Conf.* 8.11.25; *Doct. christ.* 3.36.54.
113. *Civ.* 13.11.
114. *Trin.* 15.16.26.
115. *Trin.* 14.19.25; 14.16.22.
116. *Trin.* 15.25.45.
117. *Trin.* 13.8.11; *Conf.* 7.20.26.

III. THE CONTINUITY OF HISTORY

1. *Civ.* pr. 1.
2. *Civ.* 16.37.
3. *Civ.* 4.7.
4. *Civ.* 5.19.
5. *Civ.* 5.21.
6. *Civ.* 7.32.
7. *Civ.* 1.35; see also chap. 6 below.
8. *Civ.* 3.18; *Trin.* 14.7.9; *Civ.* 10.23.
9. *Civ.* 18.44.
10. *Trin.* 4.27.23 (Acts 17:28).
11. *Trin.* 4.16.21.
12. *Civ.* 15.1.
13. *Civ.* 16.43.
14. *Trin.* 14.8.11.
15. *Trin.* 15.12.21.
16. *Civ.* 18.8–12.
17. *Trin.* 8.4–5.7.
18. *Civ.* 21.6; 18.40.
19. *Conf.* 3.7.13–14.
20. *Civ.* 11.6.
21. *Civ.* 12.12; 21.23; 22.1.
22. *Civ.* 20.1; 20.23; 16.26.
23. *Trin.* 3.2.7; *Civ.* 12.4–5.
24. *Civ.* 11.10; 11.21.
25. *Civ.* 9.1; 8.6.
26. *Civ.* 11.4–5.
27. *Civ.* 12.15.

28. Ap. *Civ.* 8.16.

29. *Civ.* 9.22.

30. *Civ.* 9.18; 10.31.

31. Ap. *Civ.* 6.5.

32. Edward Gibbon, *The History of the Decline and Fall of the Roman Empire,* chap. 2.

33. Ap. *Civ.* 6.4.

34. Ap. *Civ.* 4.31.

35. *Civ.* 3.12.

36. *Civ.* 4.30.

37. *Civ.* 4.9; 8.27.

38. *Civ.* 6.8; 6.1.

39. *Civ.* 2.13.

40. *Civ.* 2.14.

41. *Civ.* 10.9.

42. Ap. *Civ.* 6.6.

43. *Civ.* 6.8.

44. *Civ.* 8.5.

45. *Civ.* 6.7; 7.23.

46. *Civ.* 6.9.

47. *Civ.* 7.27.

48. *Civ.* 15.20.

49. *Civ.* 18.2.

50. *Civ.* 12.27.

51. *Civ.* 18.1.

52. *Civ.* 6.4.

53. *Civ.* 1. pr.

54. *Civ.* 17.20; 11.28.

55. *Conf.* 12.15.20.

56. *Civ.* 5.17.

57. *Civ.* 3.31; 4.29.

58. *Conf.* 6.11.19; *Civ.* 2.29.

59. *Civ.* 18.49.

60. *Civ.* 6.9.

61. *Civ.* 14.11.

62. *Civ.* 17.5.

63. *Civ.* 15.1.

64. *Civ.* 17.14; 17.20.

65. *Civ.* 18.45.

66. *Civ.* 17.2.

67. *Civ.* 18.28.

68. *Civ.* 17.10; 17.7.

69. *Civ.* 16.21.

70. *Civ.* 18.41.

71. *Civ.* 18.2; 18.22.

72. *Civ.* 2.21.

73. Sallust *Catiline* 7 ap. *Civ.* 5.12.

74. *Civ.* 2.21.

75. *Civ.* 3.16; 5.14.

76. *Civ.* 3.14.

77. *Civ.* 2.21.

78. *Civ.* 1.30.

79. *Civ.* 5.18.

80. *Civ.* 19.21; 19.24.

81. *Civ.* 2.2.

82. *Civ.* 18.45; 19.7.

83. *Civ.* 4.4.

84. *Civ.* 4.6.

85. *Civ.* 3.30; 3.28.

86. Horace *Ars poetica* 173.

87. Ap. *Civ.* 1.3.

88. *Civ.* 4.28.

89. *Civ.* 1.3.

90. *Civ.* 2.6–7.

91. *Civ.* 5.21.

92. *Civ.* 4.2; 5.13.

93. *Civ.* 16.10; 19.7.

94. *Civ.* 16.11; 19.7 (Eph. 4:3); for a quite different use of Ephesians 4:3, see p. 63 below.

95. *Civ.* 11.10.

96. *Civ.* 12.21.

97. *Civ.* 13.19.

98. *Civ.* 13.3; 13.14; 4.1.

99. *Conf.* 13.17.20; *Civ.* 15.17.
100. *Civ.* 15.4.
101. *Civ.* 5.1.
102. *Conf.* 7.6.8.
103. *Civ.* 16.23.
104. *Civ.* 5.1.
105. *Civ.* 5.8.
106. *Civ.* 5.9–10.
107. *Civ.* 12.13.

108. *Civ.* 12.19.
109. *Civ.* 21.17; 22.12.
110. *Civ.* 12.17–20.
111. *Civ.* 10.14.
112. *Civ.* 5.9.
113. *Civ.* 18.11.
114. *Civ.* 22.30.
115. *Civ.* 3.18.
116. *Civ.* 4.33.

IV. THE CONTINUITY OF DIVINE BEING

1. *Conf.* 13.29.44; *Trin.* 14.7.10.
2. *Trin.* 1.1.3.
3. *Trin.* 4.18.24.
4. *Trin.* 4.16.21.
5. *Trin.* 4.20.27 (2 Tim. 3:16); see also *Trin.* 4.12.15.
6. *Trin.* 5.1.2.
7. Thomas Aquinas *Summa Theologica* I.q.2.a.3, quoting *Enchir.* 11.
8. *Trin.* 15.4.6; *Conf.* 10.6.9.
9. *Conf.* 6.5.7.
10. *Trin.* 8.7.11.
11. *Trin.* 10.3.5.
12. *Civ.* 19.18.
13. *Civ.* 11.26.
14. *Trin.* 10.10.14; 15.12.21.
15. *Trin.* 8.3.4.
16. *Trin.* 8.3.5.
17. *Trin.* 4.6.10.
18. *Trin.* 1.1.1.
19. *Trin.* 1.4.7; *Civ.* 20.1; see also pp. 3–4 above.
20. *Trin.* 15.28.51.

21. *Trin.* 6.3.5.
22. *Civ.* 21.17; *Trin.* 2.9.16.
23. *Civ.* 19.3.
24. *Civ.* 10.23.
25. *Trin.* 15.28.51.
26. *Trin.* 2.pr.; *Civ.* 12.15.
27. F. C. Burkitt, "St. Augustine's Bible and the *Itala*," *Journal of Theological Studies* 11 (1910): 258–68, 447–58.
28. *Trin.* 15.2.2; 8.5.8.
29. *Trin.* 15.1.1.
30. *Trin.* 8.4.6; 8.pr.1; 7.6.12; 6.10.12.
31. *Trin.* 9.1.1.
32. *Trin.* 9.12.18.
33. *Trin.* 7.4.7; 5.3.4.
34. *Trin.* 9.11.16; see also *Serm. mont.* 4.12 and *Ep. Joh.* 4.6.
35. *Trin.* 15.2.2.
36. *Trin.* 8.2.3.
37. *Conf.* 10.6.9.
38. *Trin.* 15.7.13; 4.21.30.
39. *Trin.* 1.1.3.
40. *Trin.* 5.8.10.

41. See *Trin.* 15.20.38.

42. *Trin.* 7.4.9; 7.6.11; 5.9.10.

43. *Trin.* 5.1.1. (1 Cor. 13:12).

44. *Trin.* 5.2.3 (Ex. 3:14).

45. *Conf.* 7.8.12.

46. *Civ.* 22.2.

47. *Trin.* 12.7.10; 2.17.31.

48. *Trin.* 15.26.45; 4.1.3.

49. *Trin.* 15.13.22.

50. *Trin.* 3.9.16.

51. *Trin.* 8.9.13.

52. *Trin.* 13.9.12; *Civ.* 12.20.

53. *Trin.* 1.1.2 (1 Tim. 6:16).

54. *Trin.* 3.11.21.

55. *Trin.* 15.7.12; 15.15.24.

56. *Trin.* 6.4.6; 5.8.9.

57. *Trin.* 5.5.6.

58. *Trin.* 6.7.8; 7.1.1.

59. *Civ.* 8.6.

60. *Trin.* 5.5.6; 7.5.10; 7.1.2.

61. *Trin.* 1.8.15.

62. *Trin.* 1.12.24 (Ps. 110:3 [Vulgate]).

63. *Trin.* 7.3.4.

64. *Trin.* 6.1.1.

65. *Civ.* 12.15.

66. On this argument in Athanasius, see Jaroslav Pelikan, *The Light of the World: A Basic Image in Early Christian Thought* (New York, 1962), p. 32.

67. *Trin.* 5.6.7. (Eph. 3:14–15 [Vulgate]).

68. *Trin.* 6.3.4.

69. *Trin.* 1.11.22 (Phil. 2:6–7).

70. *Trin.* 2.10.17; 2.17.28; 4. 19.25.

71. *Trin.* 1.13.28–29.

72. *Trin.* 1.9.18 (1 Cor. 15:24).

73. *Trin.* 6.5.7 (1 John 4:8).

74. *Civ.* 11.24.

75. *Trin.* 6.5.7 (Eph. 4:3).

76. *Trin.* 15.26.47.

77. See Pelikan, *The Christian Tradition*, 2:183–98.

78. *Trin.* 8.7.10.

79. *Trin.* 8.7.10; 8.8.12.

80. See Jaroslav Pelikan, "The Doctrine of the Image of God," in *The Common Christian Roots of the European Nations: An International Colloquium in the Vatican* (Florence, 1982), 1:53–62.

81. *Trin.* 1.7.14; 6.2.3. (Gen. 1:26).

82. *Trin.* 12.6.6.

83. *Trin.* 7.6.12.

84. *Trin.* 12.5.5.

85. *Conf.* 13.11.12.

86. *Civ.* 11.28.

87. *Trin.* 12.7.12 (Eph. 4:23–24; Col. 3:9–10).

88. *Civ.* 22.24; 19.15.

89. *Trin.* 12.4.4; 11.1.1.

90. *Civ.* 22.16 (Rom. 8:29); *Trin.* 11.5.8.

91. *Trin.* 8.10.14.

92. *Trin.* 9.2.2.

93. *Trin.* 10.11.18; 14.6.8.

94. *Trin.* 10.11.18.

95. *Trin.* 11.3.6.

96. *Trin.* 11.7.11–12.

97. *Trin.* 15.7.12.

98. *Civ.* 20.15 (Rev. 22:19).

99. *Civ.* 17.12.

100. *Trin.* 15.7.12.

101. *Conf.* 10.25.36.

102. *Trin.* 14.12.16–13.17.

103. *Trin.* 14.3.4–5; 14.12.15.

104. *Trin.* 7.3.4.

105. *Trin.* 13.19.24; 13.1.4 (John 1:1, 14).

106. *Trin.* 3.11.25; 4.21.30; 2. 6.11.

107. *Trin.* 2.5.9. (John 1:14; Gal. 4:4).

108. See pp. 32–33 above.

109. *Trin.* 5.8.9; 5.16.17.

V. NATURE AND GRACE IN CONTINUITY AND DISCONTINUITY

1. *Civ.* 7.3.

2. See Pelikan, *The Christian Tradition,* 1:278–92.

3. Pelikan, *The Christian Tradition,* 4:224–25.

4. Albert H. Newman, *The Nicene and Post-Nicene Fathers of the Church,* 1st ser. 4:102n.

5. For Augustine's own use of this distinction, see, for example, *Mor. Cath.* 16.27.

6. See *Oxford Latin Dictionary* (1982), s.v. "essentia."

7. *Mor. Manich.* 2.2.

8. *Ep. fund.* 27.29; 35.39.

9. *Nat. bon.* 1; *Ep. fund.* 33.36.

10. *Nat. bon.* 3.

11. *Mor. Manich.* 6.8; 7.9.

12. *Ep. fund.* 29.32.

13. *Mor. Cath.* 13.23.

14. On the use of Ex. 3:14 in the early Christian fathers, see Pelikan, *The Christian Tradition,* 1:54.

15. *Nat. bon.* 19; see also p. 59 above.

16. *Mor. Manich.* 11.24.

17. *Ep. fund.* 37.43.

18. *Mor. Manich.* 4.6.

19. *Nat. bon.* 32.

20. *Mor. Cath.* 10.16.

21. *Mor. Cath.* 12.20; also *Anim.* 1.19.32.

22. *Nat. bon.* 35.

23. *Fort.* 13.

24. *Ep. fund.* 37.43.

25. Ap. *Faust.* 31.4 (Gen. 1:31).

26. Gen. 1:26–27.

27. Ap. *Faust.* 24.1 (Col. 3:10).

28. *Faust.* 24.2.

29. Tertullian *Against Marcion* 1.2.1–2.

30. *Mor. Manich.* 2.2.

31. *Ep. fund.* 34.38.

32. *Duab. anim.* 7.9.

33. *Fort.* 15; 17; 20–21; 25.

34. *Duab. anim.* 11.15.

35. *Fort.* 22.

36. *Mor. Cath.* 22.40.

37. *Fort.* 22.

38. *Ep. fund.* 37.43.

39. Ap. *Faust.* 24.1.

40. *Mor. Manich.* 15.36–37.

41. *Mor. Manich.* 16.49.

42. *Mor. Cath.* 27.52.

43. *Mor. Cath.* 4.6–5.7.

44. *Mor. Cath.* 35.79 (1 Cor. 7:14).

45. H. L. Mencken, *A New Dictionary of Quotations on Historical Principles* (New York, 1942), p. 194.

46. See, for example, Irenaeus *Against Heresies* 1.1.12.

47. *Fort.* 3.

48. *Mor. Manich.* 19.67–20.75.

49. *Nat. bon.* 47.

50. *Mor. Manich.* 20.74.

51. *Mor. Cath.* 1.2.

52. *Mor. Manich.* 13.27.

53. *Mor. Cath.* 31.66–67.

54. *Mor. Cath.* 35.77–78 (1 Cor. 7:31).

55. *Mor. Cath.* 17.31.

56. For example, ap. *Gest Pelag.* 20.44.

57. *Conf.* 10.37.60.

58. *Persev.* 20.53.

59. *Gest. Pelag.* 30.55.

60. See Pelikan, *The Christian Tradition,* 1:313–31.

61. *Pelag.* 2.1.1–2.2.4.

62. *Pelag.* 4.1.1.

63. *Ep.* 143.5.

64. For example, *Anim.* 19.33, written in 419.

65. *Fort.* 16–17 (Eph. 2:3).

66. *Pecc. merit.* 1.21.29; 1.27.46.

67. *Duab. anim.* 7.9.

68. *Perf. just.* 2.2–3.

69. *Nupt. concup.* 2.8.20.

70. For example, *Conf.* 11.27.35.

71. *Nat. grat.* 34.39.

72. Thomas Aquinas *Summa Theologica* I.q.74.a.2.

73. *Gen. litt.* 4.26.33.

74. *Nupt. concup.* 1.17.19.

75. *Nupt. concup.* 1.1.1.

76. *Gen. litt.* 11.1.3 (Gen. 2:25).

77. *Pecc. merit.* 2.22.36.

78. *Civ.* 14.23.

79. *Corrept.* 7.12.

80. *Nat. grat.* 24.26.

81. See Pelikan, *The Christian Tradition,* 1:289–90.

82. *Enchir.* 14.48.

83. *Nupt. concup.* 1.11.12–13.

84. *Pelag.* 4.5.9.

85. *Nupt. concup.* 1.16.18.

86. Ap. *Pelag.* 4.10.

87. See *Pelag.* 3.7.20.

88. *Faust.* 15.8.

89. *Ep.* 177.5.

90. *Faust.* 8.2.

91. *Gest. Pelag.* 5.14–15.

92. *Pelag.* 3.13.

93. *Pecc. orig.* 2.26.30.

94. *Pelag.* 1.21.39.

95. *Civ.* 22.30.

96. *Pelag.* 4.6.12.

97. *Duab. anim.* 10.13–14.

98. Ap. *Perf. just.* 6.12.

99. *Spir. litt.* 33.58.

100. *Corrept.* 11.31.

101. *Grat.* 4.7.

102. Ap. *Pelag.* 4.7.18.

103. *Nat. grat.* 44.51.

104. *Perf. just.* 19.42.

105. *Pelag.* 3.5.15–3.7.22 (Phil. 3:12).

106. *Pelag.* 1.6.12.

107. *Spir. litt.* 1.1 (Rom. 8:3).

108. *Nat. grat.* 36.42.

109. Pelikan, *The Christian Tradition,* 3:171; 4:44–50.

110. *Pelag.* 3.4.11.

111. *Fort.* 22.

112. *Ep. fund.* 37.43.

VI. THE CHURCH AS TEMPORAL AND ETERNAL

1. F. Van der Meer, *Augustine the Bishop,* trans. Brian Battershaw and G. R. Lamb (New York, 1961), p. 570.

2. *Conf.* 5.13.23.

3. *Ep.* 232.3.

4. *Ep.* 21.1.

5. *Civ.* 18.49.

6. *Mor. Cath.* 30.62–64; 29.61.

7. *Gest. Pelag.* 19.43; 35.66.

8. *Ep.* 21.1.

9. *Ep.* 53.2 (Matt. 16:18).

10. *Ep.* 209, written in 423.

11. Brown, *Augustine of Hippo,* p. 274.

12. Jerome *Apology against Rufinus* 3.6.

13. *Ep.* 28.2.

14. *Ep.* 67.1.

15. *Ep.* 72.1.1; 72.3.5.

16. *Bapt.* 1.1.1; 6.2.3.

17. *Ep.* 53.3.

18. Pelikan, *The Christian Tradition,* 1:108–20.

19. *Fid. symb.* 1.1.

20. J. N. D. Kelly, Introduction to Rufinus, *A Commentary on the Apostles' Creed,* "Ancient Christian Writers" (Westminster, Md., 1955), p. 13.

21. Rufinus *Commentary on the Apostles' Creed* 2.

22. *Bapt.* 5.26.37, quoting Cyprian *Epistle* 74.10.

23. John Henry Newman, *Apologia Pro Vita Sua,* ed. Martin J. Svaglic (Oxford, 1967), pp. 110 and 543–44n.

24. *Parm.* 3.3. (Newman's translation).

25. *Persev.* 23.65.

26. *Faust.* 11.2.

27. Aristotle *Prior Analytics* 2.5 (57b.17).

28. Aristotle *Posterior Analytics* 1.3 (72b–73a).

29. *Ev. Joh.* 78.3.

30. *Petil.* 2.61.138.

31. *Nat. grat.* 61.71.

32. Pelikan, *The Christian Tradition,* 4:125–26; 4:263–64.

33. *Ep. fund.* 5.6.

34. *Doct. christ.* 8.12.

35. *Gen. litt.* 1.1.

36. *Doct. christ.* 3.2.

37. *Jul. op. imperf.* 1.107.

38. *Trin.* 1.7.14.

39. See Jaroslav Pelikan, *Development of Christian Doctrine:*

Some Historical Prolegomena (New Haven, 1969), pp. 123–25.

40. *Bapt.* 4.3.5 (Rom. 8:29).

41. *Bapt.* 5.27.38.

42. *Bapt.* 4.3.5 (Song of Sol. 6:9).

43. *Corrept.* 15.46.

44. *Perf. just.* 15.35 (Rom. 8:30).

45. *Pelag.* 4.7.17 (Eph. 5:27).

46. *Corrept.* 9.22.

47. *Pelag.* 1.1.1.

48. *Persev.* 16.39.

49. *Persev.* 22.62.

50. *Anim.* 3.10.13.

51. *Persev.* 21.56.

52. *Corrept.* 9.21.

53. *Civ.* 15.1.

54. *Civ.* 1.35.

55. *Civ.* 5.21; see p. 47 above.

56. Heinrich Scholz, *Glaube und Unglaube in der Weltgeschichte*, p. 109.

57. *Civ.* 20.9.

58. *Civ.* 8.11; see also pp. 14–16 above.

59. *Civ.* 2.14.

60. Thomas L. Pangle, "Interpretive Essay," in his translation of *The Laws of Plato* (New York, 1980), pp. 376–77 (*Republic* 592a–b).

61. *Civ.* 8.3.

62. *Civ.* 18.50.

63. *Bapt.* 1.10.14.

64. See Scholz, *Glaube und Unglaube*, pp. 197–235.

VII. THE CONTINUITY OF THE *COMMUNIO SANCTORUM*

1. I have considered some of the issues in this chapter in my book *The Finality of Jesus Christ in an Age of Universal History* (London, 1965), pp. 31–37.

2. Pelikan, *The Christian Tradition*, 3:232–43; 4:85–98, 316–19.

3. Ap. *Petil.* 2.106.240.

4. *Petil.* 2.74.164.

5. See *Fid. symb.* 10.21; *Symb.* 14.

6. J. N. D. Kelly, *Early Christian Creeds* (London, 1950), pp. 388–97.

7. *Ps.* 149.2.

8. See the profound and provocative critique of such a reading in Krister Stendahl, *Paul among Jews and Gentiles* (Philadelphia, 1976), pp. 1–77.

9. Johannes Quasten, *Patrology* (Westminster, Md., 1951–), 1:202.

10. Justin Martyr *Dialogue with Trypho* 119 (Isa. 62:12).

11. Matt. 3:9; cf. *Corrept.* 13.39 for Augustine's predestinarian use of this passage.

12. *Bapt.* 1.15.24.

13. *Mend.* 27 (Acts 23:3).

14. *Petil.* 2.30.69 (Ps. 132:9; John 11:51).

15. Ap. *Petil.* 2.51.117 (Ps. 1:1).

16. *Petil.* 2.51.118; *Bapt.* 4.11.18; *Petil.* 3.50.62 (Matt. 23:2–3).

17. Acts 2:42 (AV).

18. Ap. *Petil.* 2.40.95 (2 Cor. 6:14).

19. Acts 5:1–10. For Augustine's reading of this case, see *Petil.* 3.48.58.

20. Jerome *Epistles* 109.3.

21. Heb. 6:4–6.

22. Jerome *Against Jovinian* 2.3.

23. Tertullian *On Modesty* 20.

24. Tertullian *On Modesty* 6.

25. Quasten, *Patrology*, 2:247.

26. W. H. C. Frend, *The Donatist Church: A Movement of Protest in Roman North Africa* (Oxford, 1952), p. 124.

27. Ap. *Bapt.* 1.1.1.

28. *Bapt.* 6.2.3.

29. Jerome *Lives of Illustrious Men* 53.

30. Edward White Benson, *Cyprian: His Life, His Times, His Work* (New York, 1897), pp. 276–79.

31. Benson's account of that development, *Cyprian*, pp. 89–106, 129–69, 222–35, written as it was by the archbishop of Canterbury, is still useful.

32. Cyprian *On the Lapsed* 15–16.

33. Cyprian *Epistles* 59.16.

34. Cyprian *Epistles* 67.2–3.

35. *Liber contra Fulgentium Donatistam* 26; translation adapted from Frend, *Donatist Church*, p. 20.

36. Ap. *Petil.* 3.51.63.

37. Ap. *Petil.* 2.11.25.

38. See *Petil.* 3.15.18.

39. Ap. *Petil.* 1.1.2; 2.3.6.

40. Ap. *Petil.* 2.20.44.

41. Ap. *Petil.* 2.9.21.

42. See p. 92 above.

43. *Petil.* 1.14.15.

44. *Petil.* 2.52.120.

45. *Ep.* 185.1.5.

46. *Petil.* 3.2.3.

47. Petil. 2.8.18; 2.21.48; 2.104.237.

48. *Petil.* 2.26.84.

49. *Petil.* 2.88.193.

50. *Petil.* 2.23.53.

51. *Petil.* 2.8.20; 2.20.45.

52. *Petil.* 2.93.205; 3.57.69.

53. *Petil.* 3.58.70.

54. *Petil.* 2.13.30; 2.15.35.

55. *Petil.* 2.32.74.

56. *Petil.* 1.22.24.

57. *Petil.* 1.13.14.

58. *Ep.* 185.4.16.

59. See p. 114 above.

60. *Bapt.* 1.18.28; 3.19.26; 5.17.23 (John 15:1–2).

61. *Bapt.* 3.2.3.

62. *Bapt.* 2.6.9.

63. Eph. 5:25–27.

64. For example, Matt. 20:28 and Phil. 2:5–11.

65. *Bapt.* 1.11.15.

66. *Bapt.* 1.17.26; 3.18.23; 4.3.5; 4.10.17; 5.16.21; 5.24.35; 5.27.38; 6.3.5; 7.10.19; 7.51.99; see also *Doct. christ.* 1.16.15.

67. *Retract.* 2.18.

68. *Gest. Pelag.* 12.27.

69. *Petil.* 3.34.39; 3.37.43.

70. *Bapt.* 4.9.14.

71. *Petil.* 3.2.3.

72. *Bapt.* 6.1.1.

73. *Petil.* 3.4.5.

74. *Petil.* 3.30.35–3.31.36.

75. *Petil.* 3.36.42.

76. *Petil.* 3.55.67.

77. *Bapt.* 3.17.22.

78. *Bapt.* 3.2.3; 2.6.8.

79. *Bapt.* 6.5.8.

80. *Bapt.* 1.18.27; 2.4.5; 3.2.5.

81. *Petil.* 2.81.178; 2.109.246.

82. *Bapt.* 3.10.15.

83. *Petil.* 3.15.18.

84. *Bapt.* 3.14.19.

85. *Bapt.* 5.20.28 (John 9:31).

86. *Bapt.* 5.7.8.

87. *Petil.* 2.105.239.

88. *Petil.* 21.23.

89. Ap. *Petil.* 2.63.141–69.153; 2.72.159 (Matt. 5:3–12).

90. Ap. *Petil.* 2.93.202.

91. *Petil.* 2.93.203.

92. *Petil.* 2.93.205; see also p. 47 above.

93. *Ep.* 185.5.19.

94. *Ep.* 185.5.20.

95. *Ep.* 185.2.8.

96. *Petil.* 2.93.212.

97. *Petil.* 2.23.52.

98. *Conf.* 10.31.45; *Bon. conjug.* 25 (Phil. 4:12).

VIII. SIGN, EVENT, AND SACRAMENT

1. *Doct. christ.* 2.41.62.

2. *Fid. symb.* 5.11.

3. *Doct. christ.* 3.11.17.

4. Ernst Cassirer, *The Philosophy of Symbolic Forms*, trans. R. Manheim, 3 vols. (New Haven, 1953–57).

5. *Oxford English Dictionary* s.v. "semantics."

6. I. L. Glatstein, "Semantics, Too, Has a Past," *Quarterly Journal of Speech* 32 (1946):48–51.

7. *Conf.* 1.17.27.

8. *Conf.* 3.4.7.

9. *Conf.* 4.2.2; 4.14.22.

10. *Conf.* 4.13.20.

11. *Civ.* 11.18.

12. *Conf.* 9.6.14.

13. See the astute comments of Paul Friedländer, *Plato: An Introduction*, trans. Hans Meyerhoff (New York, 1958), pp. 154–70.

14. See C. K. Ogden and I. A. Richards, *The Meaning of Meaning* (New York, 1923).

15. *Mag.* 5.14.

16. *Mag.* 4.9.

17. *Mag.* 3.5–6.

18. *Mag.* 7.20.

19. *Mag.* 2.3.

20. *Mag.* 9.25.

21. *Mag.* 1.2.

22. *Mag.* 11.36.

23. *Mag.* 1.2.

24. *Mag.* 11.38 (1 Cor. 1:24).

25. *Mag.* 14.46 (Matt. 23:10).

26. Plotinus *Enneads* 4.6.3.

27. *Conf.* 7.9.13–14 (John 1:1, 14); see also p. 15 above.

28. *Doct. christ.* 1.12.11.

29. *Doct. christ.* 1.13.12.

30. *Doct. christ.* 1.2.2.

31. *Doct. christ.* 2.1.1.

32. *Doct. christ.* 2.1.2.

33. *Doct. christ.* 2.2.3.

34. *Conf.* 8.12.29.

35. *Doct. christ.* 2.24.37.

36. See *Mag.* 4.7.

37. *Doct. christ.* 2.25.38.

38. *Doct. christ.* 2.38.56.

39. Martin C. D'Arcy, "The Philosophy of St. Augustine," in *Saint Augustine* (Cleveland, 1957), p. 169.

40. *Doct. christ.* 2.38.56.

41. *Lib. arb.* 2.8.22.

42. *Trin.* 4.4.7.

43. *Serm. mont.* 1.4.12.

44. *Ps.* 6.2.

45. *Civ.* 12.18.

46. *Doct. christ.* 2.39.58.

47. *Doct. christ.* 2.38.56.

48. *Doct. christ.* 2.21.32; see also p. 49 above.

49. *Doct. christ.* 2.16.25.

50. F. C. Burkitt, ed., *The Book of Rules of Tyconius* (Cambridge, 1894).

51. *Doct. christ.* 3.35.50.

52. *Doct. christ.* 3.36.52.

53. For one such difficulty, see *Civ.* 15.10–13.

54. For example, *Cons. ev.* 2.18.42.

55. See pp. 32–33 above.

56. *Doct. christ.* 3.36.54.

57. *Doct. christ.* 2.16.25.

58. See, for example, *Doct. christ.* 1.38.42.

59. *Doct. christ.* 3.10.15.

60. *Doct. christ.* 1.35.39.

61. *Doct. christ.* 2.25.39.

62. *Doct. christ.* 2.27.41.

63. *Doct. christ.* 2.28.44.

64. *Doct. christ.* 3.12.20; 3.18.26–27.

65. *Bon. conjug.* 33.

66. *Doct. christ.* 3.12.19.

67. *Doct. christ.* 3.12.20.

68. See pp. 37–38 above.

69. *Doct. christ.* 3.14.22.

70. *Doct. christ.* 3.5.9.

71. *Doct. christ.* 3.6.10.

72. *Doct. christ.* 3.7.11.

73. *Doct. christ.* 3.8.12.

74. *Doct. christ.* 3.9.13.

75. *Serm.* 228.3.

76. Pelikan, *The Christian Tradition*, 3:209–10.

77. Franciscus Moriones, ed., *Enchiridion Theologicum Sancti Augustini* (Madrid, 1961), p. 553n.

78. *Petil.* 2.30.68–69; see pp. 109–10, 119–21 above.

79. *Bapt.* 4.2.2.

80. *Nupt. concup.* 1.20.22.

81. *Bapt.* 5.12.14.

82. Rom. 6:3–4, 9–10.

83. *Petil.* 2.7.15.

84. *Spir. litt.* 6.10.

85. *Ep.* 98.9.

86. *Doct. christ.* 3.5.9.

87. John 6:53.

88. *Doct. christ.* 3.16.24.

89. *Ev. Joh.* 25.12.

90. Pelikan, *The Christian Tradition,* 4:196–97.

91. *Doct. christ.* 2.41.62.

IX. CONCLUSION: CONTINUITY WITH AUGUSTINE

1. Alfred North Whitehead, *Process and Reality*, reprint ed. (New York, 1960), p. 63.

2. Albert C. Outler, Introduction, p. 15.

3. Etienne Gilson, *Heloise and Abelard*, trans. L. K. Shook (Ann Arbor, Mich., 1960), p. 6.

4. See Jaroslav Pelikan, "A First-Generation Anselmian, Guibert of Nogent," in *Continuity and Discontinuity in Church History*, ed. F. Forrester Church and Timothy George (Leiden, 1979), pp. 71–82.

5. V. L. Bullough, "Guibert of Nogent," *New Catholic Encyclopedia*.

6. *The Autobiography of Guibert, Abbot of Nogent-sous-Coucy*, trans. C. C. S. Bland (New York, 1926).

7. Karl Barth, *Protestant Thought: From Rousseau to Ritschl*, introduction by Jaroslav Pelikan (New York, 1959), p. 93.

8. Giulio Agusto Levi, "Pensiero classico e pensiero cristiano nel 'Secretum' e nella 'Familiari' de Petrarca," *Atene e Roma* 35 (1933): 65–66.

9. Pelikan, *The Christian Tradition*, 4:19–21.

10. Outler, Introduction, p. 15.

11. Charles Norris Cochrane, *Thucydides and the Science of History* (Oxford, 1929).

12. Cochrane, *Christianity and Classical Culture*, pp. 468–69.

13. Cochrane, *Christianity and Classical Culture*, pp. 474, 484.

14. Georg Wilhelm Friedrich Hegel, *Philosophy of History*, Introduction, part 3.

15. Hegel, *Philosophy of History*, part 3, chap. 3.

16. Friedrich Engels, Preface of 30 January 1888 to *The Communist Manifesto*.

17. Etienne Gilson, "Pourquoi saint Thomas a critiqué saint Augustin," *Archives d'Histoire Doctrinale et Littéraire du Moyen Age* 1 (1926):5–127.

18. H. R. Patch, *The Tradition of Boethius: A Study of His Importance in Medieval Culture* (New York, 1935).

19. Boethius *On the Trinity*, preface.

20. Etienne Gilson, *L'esprit de la philosophie médiévale*, 2d ed. (Paris, 1944), p. 210.

21. Etienne Gilson, *Dante and Philosophy*, trans. David Moore (New York, 1949), p. 93.

22. Thomas G. Bergin, *Dante* (New York, 1965), p. 62; Dante *Inferno* 5.123.

23. Thomas Aquinas *Summa Theologica* I.q.1.a.7.

24. Benjamin Breckenridge Warfield, *Calvin and Augustine* (Philadelphia, 1956), p. 322.

25. *Ep. fund.* 5; see pp. 96–98 above.

26. John 3:8.

27. John 3:5.

28. *Ev. Joh.* 11.7; 12.5.

29. Cf. Pelikan, *The Christian Tradition*, 4:224–27.

30. John Calvin *Institutes of the Christian Religion* iv.1.1.

31. Possidius *Life of Augustine* 11.

32. Hans-Georg Beck, *Kirche und theologische Literatur im byzantinischen Reich* (Munich, 1959), pp. 686–87.

33. Jean Daniélou, *Origen*, trans. Walter Mitchell (New York, 1955), p. 310.

34. Pelikan, *The Christian Tradition*, 1:337–38.

35. Frederick H. Dudden, *Gregory the Great: His Place in History and Thought*, 2 vols. (London, 1905), 2:294.

36. Pelikan, *The Christian Tradition*, 3:50–105.

37. Daniel Angelo Philip Callus, *The Condemnation of St. Thomas at Oxford*, 2d ed. (London, 1955), p. 4.

38. Etienne Gilson, *Etudes sur le rôle de la pensée médiévale dans la formation du systéme cartésien* (Paris, 1930).

39. Hans von Campenhausen, *Men Who Shaped the Western Church*, trans. Manfred Hoffmann (New York, 1964), p. 183.

BIBLIOGRAPHY ❧

This is, of course, not even an attempt at a thorough bibliography on the thought of Augustine, but only a listing of some of the works consulted or cited most often here. Many of these works, in turn, contain more detailed bibliographies of their own. For books cited en passant in the body of this monograph, I have provided bibliographical information in the notes and have not repeated it here.

Alfaric, Prosper. *L'évolution intellectuelle de Saint Augustin.* Paris, 1918.

Andresen, C. *Zum Augustingespräch der Gegenwart.* Darmstadt, 1962.

Angus, Samuel. *The Sources of the First Ten Books of Augustine's* De Civitate Dei. Princeton, 1906.

Armstrong, A. Hilary, ed. *The Cambridge History of Ancient and Early Medieval Philosophy.* Cambridge, 1967.

Battenhouse, Roy W., ed. *A Companion to the Study of St. Augustine.* Oxford, 1955.

Benz, Ernst. *Marius Victorinus und die Entwicklung der abendländischen Willensmetaphysik.* Stuttgart, 1932.

Bonner, Gerald. *St. Augustine of Hippo: Life and Controversies.* London, 1963.

Bourke, Vernon J. *Augustine's Quest for Wisdom.* Milwaukee, 1945.

Boyer, Charles. *Christianisme et Néoplatonisme dans la formation de S. Augustin.* 2d ed. Rome, 1953.

Brown, Peter. *Augustine of Hippo: A Biography.* London, 1967.

Burnaby, John. *Amor Dei: A Study of the Religion of St. Augustine.* London, 1938.

Chevalier, Irenée. *Saint Augustin et la pensée grecque: Les relations trinitaires.* Fribourg, 1940.

Cochrane, Charles Norris. *Christianity and Classical Culture: A Study of Thought and Action from Augustus to Augustine.* London, 1944.

Courcelle, Pierre. *Recherches sur les Confessions de saint Augustin.* Paris, 1950.

————. *Les Confessions de saint Augustin dans la tradition littéraire: Antécédents et postérité.* Paris, 1963.

Cullman, Oscar. *Christ and Time.* Trans. by Floyd V. Filson. 2d ed. Philadelphia, 1964.

Dinkler, Erich. *Die Anthropologie Augustins.* Stuttgart, 1934.

Figgis, John Neville. *The Political Aspects of S. Augustine's* City of God. London, 1921.

Fortin, Ernest L. *Christianisme et la culture philosophique au Ve siècle.* Paris, 1959.

Gilson, Etienne. *The Christian Philosophy of Saint Augustine.* New York, 1960.

Henry, Paul. *Plotin et l'Occident.* Louvain, 1934.

Kaiser, Hermann-Josef. *Augustinus—Zeit und Memoria.* Bonn, 1969.

Kretschmar, Georg. *Studien zur frühchristlichen Trinitätstheologie.* Tübingen, 1956.

Kretzmann, Norman, ed. *Infinity and Continuity in Ancient and Medieval Thought.* Ithaca, N.Y., 1982.

Ladner, Gerhart B. *The Idea of Reform: Its Impact on Christian Thought and Action in the Age of the Fathers.* Cambridge, Mass., 1959.

Lechner, Odilo. *Idee und Zeit in der Metaphysik Augustins*. Munich, 1964.

Marrou, Henri Irenée. *Saint Augustine and His Influence through the Ages*. Trans. by P. Hepburne-Scott. London, 1957.

Nygren, Anders. *Agape and Eros*. Trans. by Philip S. Watson. Philadelphia, 1953.

Nygren, Gotthard. *Das Prädestinationsproblem in der Theologie Augustins*. Lund, 1956.

O'Donovan, O. *The Problem of Self-Love in St. Augustine*. New Haven, 1980.

O'Meara, John J. *The Young Augustine*. London, 1954.

Outler, Albert C. Introduction to *Confessions and Enchirdion*. Philadelphia, 1955.

Pelikan, Jaroslav. *The Christian Tradition: A History of the Development of Doctrine*. Chicago, 1971–.

Portalié, Eugène. *A Guide to the Thought of Saint Augustine*. Trans. by R. J. Bastian. Chicago, 1960.

Ratzinger, Joseph. *Volk und Haus Gottes in Augustins Lehre von der Kirche*. Munich, 1954.

Reuter, Hermann. *Augustinische Studien*. Gotha, 1887.

Schindler, Alfred. *Wort und Analogie in Augustins Trinitätslehre*. Tübingen, 1965.

Schmaus, Michael. *Die psychologische Trinitätslehre des heiligen Augustinus*. Münster, 1927.

Scholz, Heinrich. *Glaube und Unglaube in der Weltgeschichte: Ein Kommentar zu Augustins* De Civitate Dei. Leipzig, 1911.

TeSelle, Eugene. *Augustine the Theologian*. New York, 1970.

Troeltsch, Ernst. *Augustin, die christliche Antike und das Mittelalter*. Munich, 1915.

Willis, Geoffrey G. *Saint Augustine and the Donatist Controversy*. London, 1950.